6/15

International Relations

A Beginner's Guide

ONEWORLD BEGINNER'S GUIDES combine an original, inventive, and engaging approach with expert analysis on subjects ranging from art and history to religion and politics, and everything in-between. Innovative and affordable, books in the series are perfect for anyone curious about the way the world works and the big ideas of our time.

aesthetics
africa
american politics
anarchism
animal behaviour
anthropology
anti-capitalism
aquinas
art
artificial intelligence
the bahai faith
the beat generation
the bible
biodiversity
bioterror & biowarfare
the brain
british politics
the Buddha
cancer
censorship
christianity
civil liberties
classical music
climate change
cloning
cold war
conservation
crimes against humanity
criminal psychology
critical thinking
daoism
democracy
descartes
dewey

dyslexia
energy
the enlightenment
engineering
epistemology
european union
evolution
evolutionary psychology
existentialism
fair trade
feminism
forensic science
french literature
french revolution
genetics
global terrorism
hinduism
history of science
homer
humanism
huxley
iran
islamic philosophy
islamic veil
journalism
judaism
lacan
life in the universe
literary theory
machiavelli
mafia & organized crime
magic
marx
medieval philosophy

middle east
modern slavery
NATO
the new testament
nietzsche
the northern ireland conflict
nutrition
oil
opera
the palestine–israeli conflict
particle physics
paul
philosophy
philosophy of mind
philosophy of religion
philosophy of science
planet earth
postmodernism
psychology
quantum physics
the qur'an
racism
reductionism
religion
renaissance art
the russian revolution
shakespeare
the small arms trade
sufism
the torah
united nations
volcanoes

International Relations

A Beginner's Guide

Charles Jones

ONEWORLD

A Oneworld Paperback Original

First published in North America, Great Britain & Australia
by Oneworld Publications, 2014

Copyright © Charles Jones 2014

The moral right of Charles Jones to be identified as the Author
of this work has been asserted by him in accordance with
the Copyright, Designs and Patents Act 1988

ISBN 978-1-78074-303-5
eISBN 978-1-78074-304-2

Typeset by Siliconchips Services Ltd, UK
Printed and bound in Denmark by
Nørhaven, Viborg

Oneworld Publications
10 Bloomsbury Street
London WC1B 3SR
England

Stay up to date with the latest books,
special offers, and exclusive content from
Oneworld with our monthly newsletter

Sign up on our website
www.oneworld-publications.com

To Linda Jones

Contents

Contents

Abbreviations

BISA	British International Studies Association
BP	British Petroleum (the abbreviated form is now the official title of the firm)
CoW	Correlates of War
DC	Developed country
DRC	Democratic Republic of Congo
EEZ	Exclusive economic zone
EU	European Union
FARC	Fuerzas Armadas de la Revolución Colombiana
FDI	Foreign direct investment
FIFA	Fédération International de Football Association
G77	Group of 77 (in UNCTAD and similar bodies)
GATT	General Agreement on Tariffs and Trade
GDP	Gross domestic product
GNP	Gross national product
HSBC	Hong Kong and Shanghai Banking Corporation (the abbreviated form is now the official title of the firm)
IFI	International Financial Institution
IGO	Intergovernmental organization
IMF	International Monetary Fund
INGO	International non-governmental organization
IP	International Politics
IPCC	Intergovernmental Panel on Climate Change
IPE	International Political Economy
IR	International Relations (the academic field)
ISA	International Studies Association

ISI	Import substituting industrialization
LDC	Less developed country
MID	Militarized Interstate Dispute
NAFTA	North American Free Trade Agreement
NATO	North Atlantic Treaty Organization
NIC	Newly industrializing country
NGO	Non-governmental organization
OAPEC	Organization of Arab Petroleum Exporting Countries
OPEC	Organization of Petroleum Exporting Countries
TNC	Transnational corporation
UK	United Kingdom of Great Britain and Northern Ireland
UN(O)	United Nations (Organization)
UNCLOS	United Nations Conference on the Law of the Sea
UNCTAD	United Nations Conference on Trade and Development
UNGA	United Nations General Assembly
UNHCR	United Nations High Commission for Refugees
UNSC	United Nations Security Council
US(A)	United States (of America)
USSR	Union of Soviet Socialist Republics (Soviet Union)
WISC	World International Studies Committee
WMD	Weapons of mass destruction
WTO	World Trade Organization

Note: Unless otherwise indicated, dollars (\$) are US dollars,
1 billion = 1,000,000,000 (1×10^9) and
1 trillion = 1,000,000,000,000 (1×10^{12}).

List of Figures

Preface

A bland introduction to any field of study without an argument to engage the attention of the reader would be very dull. This book has two.

The first is that International Relations deserves attention precisely because it is not a discipline marked off from other fields by its subject matter or method; nor is it a sub-discipline of political science. I have taken care to provide a basic outline of the growth of the modern states-system and the world economy, the rise of international organizations of every sort, and some principal tendencies in global society. However, social sciences such as economics or politics that begin by abstracting their subject matter from society as a whole in order to apply a distinctive method run a serious risk of losing in relevance what they gain in elegance. The messier, more eclectic approach of International Relations looks not only to history, economics, politics, and law – its old companions – but beyond them to social anthropology, sociology, and literary and cultural studies. It is perhaps closer in spirit to its purer cousins, contemporary laboratory sciences, where it is commonplace for investigators faced with a new problem to seek new techniques and new kit to tackle it.

The second argument is a call to resist the frequently drawn contrast between political realism and liberal internationalism. This continues to be widely regarded as the principal theoretical division of the field, even though many have challenged it. Realists and liberals are generally said to differ in world view and in their typical policy recommendations. Realists are a pessimistic bunch, at best doubtful about the prospects for international co-operation and progress. Liberals, by contrast, are generally said to be more optimistic (or credulous). Setting aside these differences in temperament, the division is better thought of as a disagreement about the appropriate scope of study. Realists, often identifying themselves with International *Politics*, opt for a narrow agenda; their critics prefer a broader one.

Anyone who embarks on the study of international relations with a realist view of the world already firmly in place will tend to restrict attention to affairs of state, and be content to privilege political science over other relevant disciplines, if not to regard International Relations as a sub-field of politics. For others, their agendas perhaps set by practical experience in the field, a broader perspective is needed, allowing a more innovative range of possible solutions to global problems such as climate change or slavery. The division between realists and liberals therefore boils down to the question of which is set first, interpretation or agenda. Support for the broad-agenda view often rests on the claim that current levels of cross-border transactions and their impact on the lives of ordinary people are unprecedented. This may be true; but the argument offered here is that the broad view has always been possible, and that the choice between realist emphasis on relations between states and a broader liberal view embracing relations between peoples has as much to do with the selection of evidence as with the extraordinary dynamics of recent decades. Attitudes and agendas can be separated, and the choice of methods of inquiry is a practical matter, not an issue of principle.

History consists of two quite different things. There is what happened in the past, and there are stories about what happened in the past. The only way of approaching the first is through the second. It is much the same with international relations. There is the complex parade of wars, negotiations, commerce, and migration across frontiers; there is also the interpretation of these events, generally concentrated in universities, business schools, military establishments, and diplomatic academies. The first of these is usually referred to as international relations – plural and lower-case – and the second – singular and with initial capitals – as International Relations, or IR for short. This book provides an introduction to both.

1
What is international relations?

Many people pay little attention to what's going on beyond their own local community. For the poorest, the world over, securing food and shelter dominates their lives. For those with means and leisure, news bulletins and foreign holidays provide windows on the wider world, but the glass can be pretty frosty.

However, year after year more and more people cross national frontiers seeking employment or sanctuary. When they do so, they are responding to the kinds of forces examined in this book, most of all market incentives and organized violence. But Colombian taxi drivers in New York, Somali refugees in London, or North European tourists in Marrakesh have little incentive to move beyond the cultural bubble formed by their compatriots in Queens, Tower Hamlets, or the hotels of the Marrakech *Palmeraie*. Cheap transport, Skype, e-mail, and access to media in other languages make it easier than ever to opt out of integration. This sort of globalization often leads to merely superficial interaction between nations.

So who really cares about international relations? Who wants to know, and why? Who *needs* to know? In the past, this was quite simple. International relations were generally understood as relations between states, conducted through their heads of state, ministries of foreign affairs, diplomatic corps, and armed forces. It followed that international relations were the business of a restricted elite of experts, generally from wealthy and powerful families, who embarked on a career in public service with a good general education, learning the crafts of statesmanship, diplomacy, and soldiering on the job. It was also assumed that each state housed one nation, for whom the state could speak with authority. Hence 'inter-*national* relations'.

There is ample reason to doubt the accuracy of this description of world politics. Many states have several distinct nations within their frontiers, keen to assert themselves in the wider world. Many are home to recently arrived communities whose members still identify with their country of origin as much as their new home, and may take an active part in its politics. Some states have a firm administrative grip on the whole of their territory; others control little beyond their seat of government, the remainder being governed by insurgent groups who effectively operate their own foreign policies. Some states maintain tight central control over external relations; others give considerable latitude to several ministries and other agencies to negotiate with their peers. Most are fully independent, but some have effectively lost sovereignty for a time following war or disaster, or else have sub-contracted some of their functions to non-governmental organizations staffed by expatriates. In short, the neat world in which professional diplomats and political leaders had exclusive command of international relations has long gone, if indeed it ever existed. Many others are now involved.

Commerce is also an important factor in international relations. Long-distance trade is as old as civilization itself, and merchants have always had a keen interest in knowing which routes were safest and which markets and commodities most profitable. More recently, cheap transport has made it commonplace to cross national frontiers in search of employment or higher education.

Many religions have spread beyond their country of origin, often following lucrative trade routes or victorious armies.

The faithful cross boundaries for religious instruction, as pilgrims, as missionaries, and to find suitable marriage partners. Religious practice around the world is sometimes enjoined by law, sometimes merely consistent with it, and sometimes at odds with it. The teachings of the Roman Catholic Church on contraception, abortion, and divorce, for example, are not reflected in French legislation any more than are the views of other faith communities on polygamy or the veiling of women. Religious leaders, like traders, have needed to understand and work within the wider world.

When journeys for leisure and business purposes are also considered, cross-frontier travel becomes a significant element in the world economy, estimated at around fourteen percent of world product.

Relations between states are no longer handled solely by heads of government and their foreign ministers. Ministries of commerce, environment, foreign aid, finance, and justice are just a few of those now dealing routinely with one another and with non-governmental organizations (NGOs), more or less independently of their countries' foreign ministries. Very often such dealings are regulated by international agreements and are routinely handled by organizations such as the United Nations, the World Trade Organization, the International Monetary Fund, and the World Bank.

Heads of government now often deal with urgent and conflictive issues by meeting face to face, a task which would once have been the province of diplomats. In some regions of the world, most notably Europe, relations between states have gone beyond co-operation to something approaching federation. This has required the creation of substantial administrative and political structures, such as the European Commission in Brussels and the parliament in Strasbourg.

Meanwhile, improvements in transport and communications have made it possible for large firms to operate globally.

Transnational corporations such as Toyota, BP (formerly British Petroleum), HSBC (formerly the Hong Kong and Shanghai Banking Corporation), or Coca Cola employ hundreds of thousands of people in dozens of countries. Strictly speaking, these firms are international non-governmental organizations (INGOs), but that phrase is more often used to describe not-for-profits such as Greenpeace, Oxfam, or Amnesty International. Finally, the world's armed forces, once exclusively devoted to defence or conquest, are now very often charged with peacekeeping, state-building, and economic development tasks in parts of the world weakened by conflict or threatened by insurgency. Officers are called upon to use political and diplomatic skills as they strive to run hospitals or airports far from home.

Whole nations feel the effects of these cross-border flows. The numbers of migrant workers and the monies they send to their countries of origin (remittances) bear witness to this, as do the residents of the world's semi-permanent refugee camps. Seeking asylum in countries less brutal than their own, refugees often experience hostility or indifference in their host countries.

Together, national politicians and civil servants with international responsibilities, the staff of international governmental organizations, entrepreneurs and managers operating across frontiers, the expatriate staff of NGOs, and the world's officer corps number hundreds of thousands if not millions. As they channel resources from one country to another and engage in humanitarian interventions and post-conflict development programmes, these people conduct international relations and grow to understand them first hand. The best justification for the academic study of international relations, as it has developed over the past century, is its provision, for these practitioners, of a coherent view of the whole complex pattern of political, social, and economic relations within which they act: a gateway into their professions or an opportunity for critical reflection on existing practice.

If the extraordinary growth in the numbers directly and practically concerned in the conduct of international relations accounts for the demand for relevant reading and degree programmes, the supply side has been driven by a different set of concerns. The motives of educators have been various. Back in the 1920s some of the founders of university departments and organizations such as the US Council on Foreign Relations believed that the lack of democratic control over foreign policy had been a leading cause of war. They hoped that more-informed publics would be able to prevent any repeat of the catastrophe of August 1914, when Europe was plunged into four years of destructive warfare. Understanding the causes of war would help avert it. More broadly, they believed that understanding global markets and Great Power politics might help those at risk from these forces to achieve some degree of independence and freedom.

That liberal belief in the value of an informed citizenry survives in the school curricula of many wealthy democracies, but its scope has widened markedly. Pupils are urged from their earliest years to think not only about war, but also climate change, ecology, and global inequality. They are encouraged to empathize with their contemporaries in the world's poorest countries. These educational initiatives, together with the public advocacy work of NGOs and the celebrity activism of George Clooney, Bono, and others, have raised public concern about foreign policy and encouraged feelings of moral responsibility. These may make it a little harder for governments to go back on their aid commitments or resort to force.

The media report daily on armed conflicts and extreme poverty, and concerned citizens in relatively wealthy and secure countries want to understand the links between these distant events and their own familiar worlds. How did cholera spread from Nepal to earthquake-stricken Haiti in 2010? What clothes and food can people buy and what journeys can they make in good conscience, sure that they are not profiting from child labour or contributing to environmental ruin? Public understanding of international relations matters, then, not just because citizens in democracies vote in governments, but because their daily private decisions have significant cumulative effects on people all over the world. Sometimes direct non-governmental global action is helped by the transnational character of its target. In July 2012 a global boycott of the Hyatt group, branded by some of its employees as the worst hotel employer in the USA, was supported by demonstrations in India, the UK, and elsewhere.

Scares over food security are a good example of governments and global businesses (in this case supermarkets) rushing to address consumer concerns because they know the electoral and market costs of a slow or inadequate response. In 1989 two Chilean grapes tainted with cyanide were discovered in a California supermarket; the USA promptly banned imports of Chilean fruit. In 2011 a premature and unjustified German claim that Spanish cucumbers were responsible for an outbreak of E. coli led to substantial losses for Spanish farmers. In 2013 governments, suppliers, and supermarkets took rapid action following the discovery of undeclared horsemeat in products on sale in Ireland and the UK. This was despite the fact that there was neither a threat to health nor any offence against religious sensibilities. In short, rising public awareness of global interconnectedness, together with sensitivity to real or imagined abuses or threats, may now have immediate and costly implications in distant places.

After primary and secondary education, the idealistic motives for the teaching and study of IR merge with the more practical needs of present and future participants in international relations. Many people working in international relations do so because they want to become global activists, trying to make the world a better place. They include not only aid workers and human rights advocates, but also those would-be bankers and soldiers who believe that economic growth will filter down to the world's poor or hold that wealth and justice are unattainable without security. Practitioners moving back into the teaching of IR, public administration, and development management encourage the spread of best practice and critical reflection among those aspiring to global careers.

The Leading Actors: States and Intergovernmental Organizations

The list of current and prospective participants in international relations includes a wide range of non-state actors, both intergovernmental and non-governmental, multipurpose and specialized. But a survey of leading actors can hardly exclude states themselves, which remain a source of welfare and mayhem. Indeed, the international organizations considered in this section and the next exist either by agreement between states or with their consent. The entire United Nations system was established by states and is funded by them. Charitable NGOs require permission to operate within the territories of states and are subject to scrutiny by state agencies. They work within parameters set by governments in both their host and home countries, the latter often among their principal donors.

States continue to maintain embassies and consulates in those countries where their firms and nationals are most active. Major states maintain armed forces able to rescue their nationals when violence flares and to participate directly in military operations when their interests are threatened, either unilaterally or as members of alliances such as NATO (the North Atlantic Treaty Organization) or the African Union. Heads of state and leading ministers meet bilaterally and in a variety of forums. Among the most important of these are the closely related G8 and the G20. The first of these is a regular meeting of the heads of government of Canada, France, Germany, Italy,

Japan, Russia, the UK, and the USA, with five additional states – Brazil, India, Mexico, the People's Republic of China, and South Africa – increasingly attending as guests. The second was at first primarily concerned with financial management, but has since transformed into an additional forum for discussion of political and security issues by the heads of government of a slightly wider circle, including Argentina, Australia, Indonesia, Saudi Arabia, South Korea, and Turkey.

States also continue to negotiate binding treaties and new conventions, often in close consultation with private interest groups and NGOs. They continue to set the terms on which firms do business within their territories and trade internationally. Some are tiny and impotent, but for the most part they are powerful and indispensable. Yet in all their external dealings and in many aspects of domestic policy, such as respect for human rights, states have progressively found themselves obliged to take heed of international organizations and international law. This is especially true when dealing with global trends – whether demographic, commercial, or environmental – that can't be dealt with by any state acting alone.

Nearly all the world's states – now approaching two hundred – belong to the United Nations Organization (UNO). Formed in 1945 as successor to the League of Nations, the UNO, more often referred to simply as the United Nations (UN), was created to maintain global peace and security. At the start there were fifty-one members, almost half of them American. As European empires were dissolved, fatally weakened by the Second World War, numerous new states were formed, chiefly in Asia and Africa. They duly joined the UN.

The chief elements of the UN are the Security Council (UNSC) and the General Assembly (UNGA). The Security Council has a restricted membership and agenda, bearing primary responsibility for averting threats to peace and security. By historical accident the five major victors of the Second

World War are permanent members, each with a veto over any significant decision. These are China, France, Russia (as successor to the Soviet Union (USSR)), the United Kingdom (UK), and the United States of America (USA). Ten states elected by the UNGA also serve two-year terms on the Security Council, with five renewed each year. During the Cold War the veto power of the permanent members effectively stymied UNSC action on any issue on which the USA and the Soviet Union disagreed, and these were numerous. The end of the Cold War brought a brief period of unanimity, during which Resolution 678 was passed, authorizing the use of force to reverse Iraq's 1990 invasion of Kuwait. As a result the USA assembled an impressive coalition to assist and legitimize a successful attack on Iraqi forces. But the moment passed, and more recent uses of force by the USA, notably the 2003 invasion of Iraq, have been less unambiguously legal and therefore less widely supported, in part for lack of clear UNSC authorization.

The General Assembly debates a wide range of topics and every member state has a single vote. Since the 1960s its voting system has secured a permanent majority for a coalition of the world's newer and poorer states. Initially referred to collectively as the Third World, because of their resistance to close alignment either with the capitalist USA or the communist USSR, these states soon began to be called the Global South. Because they were no longer distinguished ideologically from the two superpowers, they were contrasted with wealthier states, which were almost exclusively located north of the tropics. Although the resolutions of the UNGA are not binding, this voting system allowed the new states to launch a North–South dialogue in the 1960s. The Cold War had been characterized as an East–West conflict; now the Global South sought to change the agenda by prioritizing national liberation and economic and social welfare over universalist ideology. One can get a sense of how the UN engages in the creation of international law and creates possibilities for the Global South to influence world politics from the history of third United Nations Conference on the Law of the Sea (UNCLOS III). This body deliberated between 1968 and 1982, producing a multilateral treaty or convention that had been ratified by 164 states by the end of 2012.

The United Nations Conference on the Law of the Sea – A Temporary International Governmental Organization

The third UN Conference on the Law of the Sea (UNCLOS III) was established in 1968, first met in 1973, and then convened periodically until 1982. The aim was to produce a convention (or multilateral treaty) covering a wide range of topics, including the definition of different categories of offshore waters, in each of which distinct laws applied, and the development of a regime to govern exploitation of seabed mineral resources. The conference created new laws, superseding or supplementing earlier conventions and codifying existing custom.

These issues were of great concern to many countries, rich and poor. A number of states had unilaterally extended their territorial waters from the traditional three miles to twelve. Several American states with rich fisheries, including Chile, Ecuador, and Peru, claimed an exclusive right to economic exploitation of waters up to 200 miles from their coasts. Even before the convention was agreed, the European Economic Community, later to become the European Union (EU), adopted the 200-mile exclusive economic zone (EEZ) as the basis for a common fisheries policy made urgent by the accession in 1973 of Denmark, Ireland, and the UK.

At a moment when prices of oil and minerals were unusually high, states lacking advanced mining industries – especially land-locked countries – feared that deep seabed mineral resources could be snatched by mining corporations from the industrialized North. They wanted to establish the principle that these resources constituted 'a common heritage of mankind'.

Three aspects of this lengthy process deserve attention. First of all, UNCLOS was, as the name suggests, a temporary organization that ceased to exist once its purpose was served. This said, it established one lasting institution, the International Seabed Authority, and affected the operations of others. Second, UNCLOS proceeded by consensus rather than by voting, a process that neutralized the permanent majority of the Global South while also creating opportunities for small states with strong diplomatic capability, such as Malta, to broker deals. Third, the United States failed to ratify the convention. Ratification is the process by which the decision of a government to sign a treaty or convention is referred to the country's legislature for approval. Powerful interests in the USA objected to the International Seabed Authority and the idea of a common heritage of humankind, and Congress refused to approve the convention.

Despite this, the convention came into force in 1994 after it had been ratified by two-thirds of the members of the UN, and the USA has largely abided by it. However, the USA has objected to Chinese attempts to extend the concept of the EEZ in such a way as to exclude US naval vessels, and former US ambassador John Bolton has counselled against ratification, since it would bring the USA under the authority of dispute settlement procedures that might assist the Chinese.

Besides its security and economic functions, the UN oversees numerous programmes and agencies, each devoted to a specific task, or function, that cannot be performed without co-operation between states. It is worth pausing for a moment on that word 'function', because it was adopted in the early twentieth century to characterize one stream of the liberal approach to international relations that was to become notable in academic IR, and most of all in the study of regional organizations such as the EU, under the title of functionalism. The idea was that states only commanded the loyalty of their citizens so long as they continued to be the sole guarantors of security and wealth. The growth of the world economy had accelerated during the later nineteenth century, following the Industrial Revolution. Improved means of transport and communication enabled still more rapid increases in international trade, investment, and migration. These in their turn began to require co-operation between states to control epidemic diseases, regulate trade in dangerous drugs, provide relief for prisoners of war, clear international payments, and manage multinational waterways such as the Danube.

Functionalists argued that this profusion of international organizations would progressively take over responsibility for the welfare of their citizens from their members. States would send representatives mandated to promote their interests, but since they would have to be competent in their respective specialized field, these representatives – whether bankers, engineers, or doctors – would be ruled by professional imperatives stronger than national loyalty. The more people saw that their welfare depended on functional international organizations, the less loyalty each would feel to his or her state, and the less inclined to fight for it. Little by little, the ability of states to mobilize their populations for war would ebb away. A tipping point would be reached, at which citizens' loyalties would shift to a higher, supranational level.

This progressive vision turned out to be over-optimistic. It all proved much more difficult than expected, partly because experts disagree, but rather more because each distinct and genuinely held technical view offers advantages and opportunities to one party or another in a political negotiation. Climate change is a prominent issue that has provoked especially intractable disagreement for these reasons, in spite of its seemingly technical nature.

Expert Opinion on Climate Change

Since the 1980s climate change has risen to prominence as an issue in global politics. It is widely thought that increasing levels of carbon dioxide and other greenhouse gases – as a result of industrial activity – have led to a warming of the earth's atmosphere. This might seem just the kind of subject on which policy-makers should consult experts. Is it really happening? Is human activity responsible? If so, is the solution reduction of emissions or adaptation to changed conditions?

It was in response to these questions that the United Nations established the Intergovernmental Panel on Climate Change in 1988. Its declared aim is 'to provide the world with a clear scientific view on the current state of knowledge on climate change and its potential environmental impacts'.

Opinion is polarized both within the scientific community and beyond. Concern about climate change first developed in industrialized European countries in the 1980s, leading to the establishment of political parties, the Greens, dedicated to environmental issues and the widespread reduction of emissions. The 1997 Kyoto protocol exposed sharp differences of opinion. Many states committed to reducing their emissions, but countries such as India and China, that had only recently embarked on rapid industrialization, objected to being told to restrict emissions by those who had created the problem in the first place. Public opinion also diverged, with many more people worrying about the issue in Europe and Japan than in China or the USA.

A sharp ideological divide opened up between those who counselled adaptation to new conditions and those who argued for reduced emissions. In the first camp were many liberals opposed to state intervention on principle and also specialist energy economists, some of whom believed that markets could resolve the issue. Against them stood a majority of the natural scientists working on climate change, who lacked confidence in adaptation. Even when experts agreed on the facts of what was happening, they disagreed about likely outcomes and appropriate remedies. Meanwhile, the resource-rich USA and global energy companies have been resistant to controls on emissions. Divergence of expert opinion has made it possible for states and companies to choose those experts most supportive of their interests, sometimes funding them, and this has led to accusations and counter-accusations of bias and poor scientific practice, undermining confidence in the IPCC.

This is only one of many instances where functionalist hopes of finding technical solutions to global problems have been frustrated by a process of politicization. Another is fisheries, where experts disagree about the best ways to preserve stocks.

Over the past century the number of international organizations has burgeoned, as predicted by the functionalists. They manage everything from the allocation of barcodes to the organization of sports tournaments. Some, such as the Organization of Islamic Cooperation, the British Commonwealth, or the Organization of Petroleum Exporting Countries (OPEC), remain outside the UN system. Within that system are organizations and funds, some antedating the establishment of the UN, with responsibility for civil aviation, the co-ordination of postal services, labour conditions, meteorology, public health, the standardization of international property law, and the welfare of women, children and refugees, to name but a few. Just as the pioneer functionalists had hoped, the headquarters of these organizations are widely dispersed to avoid any possible replication of untrustworthy and bellicose statehood.

Regional organizations are a second important class of IGO. For a time they became the darlings of functionalist political scientists in spite of their tendency to concentrate authority rather than disperse it. Initially, modern state-builders preferred a federal model. Throughout the long process of decolonization, European powers and their successor states in the Americas tried to ensure the viability of new polities with federal constitutional arrangements. The most spectacular success, though only after much bloodshed in the 1860s, was the United States of America. South Africa (1910) was also costly, the fruit of two wars. Canada (1867) and Australia (1901) proved easier. Most of these federal constitutions were imposed, but none could have survived without general consent. Elsewhere the record was poor. None of the Spanish viceroyalties survived the wars of independence intact; the British left only a cricket team and a university in the West Indies and even less in Central and East Africa, in each of which they had aspired to create a federal state.

Since 1945 the federal model has fallen out of favour and instead the major successes of regionalism have involved the co-operation and gradual integration of groups of neighbouring states with distinct histories and cultures and longstanding animosities. These have included Spanish and Portuguese speakers in MERCOSUR (or MERCOSUL), unconquered Thais together with the peoples of formerly British, Dutch, and US dependencies in the Association of South East Asian Nations (ASEAN), and most of all the warring and culturally diverse states of Europe, now largely united in the EU.

All these organizations are very different one from another. To study them at all closely is to learn the difference between co-operation and integration. But each was above all the solution to a strategic problem, and each achieved its primary political objective. MERCOSUR has been part of a more general rapprochement between two adjacent rivals as they pass each other on the moving stairway of economic fortune, Brazil heading up and Argentina down. ASEAN, though formed in 1967, only came into its own a decade later as a demonstration of international co-operation calculated to restrain a militarily formidable Vietnam, following the 1973 defeat of US forces. The EU, originally known as the European Common Market, was formed in 1957 by the Treaty of Rome. Its purpose was very much the same as that of NATO. In the words of its first secretary general, Lord Ismay, this was 'to keep the Russians out, the Americans in, and the Germans down'. Together, the two organizations pulled off the trick nicely. Though the USA is not a member of the EU, the common market created by the original six member states provided an enlarged market that attracted substantial investment from US multinational firms. The new European institutions facilitated a rapid recovery of German industrial strength that did not threaten its neighbours, and an economic model that soon showed itself superior to Soviet planning.

With its council, parliament, and court, together with free movement of labour, direct application of some legislation, and a currency shared by many of its member states, the EU is the most integrated of today's regional organizations. Yet as a political experiment it remains inconclusive, and this has been an important element in its success. It was conceived by some of its founders as a federation in the making. Others saw it as a functionalist initiative designed to take power out of the hands of national governments that had twice in a generation tumbled into war. Neo-functionalists maintained that integration that began with relatively uncontroversial or technical co-operation would culminate, through successive crises, in political union. For a third group the EU allowed co-operation between post-imperial nations that were only able to maintain their position in a world of emergent economic giants by pooling their resources. Institutional and political development has been carefully regulated to minimize conflict between these groups, provide a strong voice in global trade negotiations, and to avoid any suggestion that they seek to match the military power of the United States.

International Non-governmental Organizations

States remain powerful actors in international relations, whether acting unilaterally, regionally, or through broader international organizations. Yet they are accompanied by a large, varied, and growing number of international non-governmental organizations that complement or challenge the activities of states. Discussion of their role in global society sometimes assumes that INGOs are exclusively campaigning, not-for-profit bodies. Substantial players based in the Global North, such as Action Aid, Amnesty, Greenpeace, Human Rights Watch, Oxfam, or Plan, raise money directly from Northern publics and also bid for funds from state development agencies. Plan-UK, for example, is a medium-sized INGO that concentrates on helping children. Of its total 2009–10 income of £50 million, £14 million came from official sources. Oxfam, a larger organization, with an income of over £200 million in 2009–10, has quite consistently raised about a quarter of its funds from governments and official agencies. But there are many other varieties of INGO. It may come as a surprise to note that the development budget of Oxfam is dwarfed by that of the Fédération Internationale de Football Association (FIFA), which generated over $1 billion in 2009–10, mostly from the sale of World Cup television rights. For FIFA, organization of the soccer World Cup is the leading priority, but its development expenditure had risen from less than $10 million a year in the late 1990s to $381 million by the end of the first decade of the new millennium; they fund turf pitches, referee training, and the creation of national leagues in sub-Saharan Africa and elsewhere. This is more than Oxfam's global spend. There is no doubting the importance of football in developing team and leadership skills among young people worldwide. Yet FIFA have recently been plagued by accusations of corruption, and there is ample room to doubt whether all the funds FIFA claims to devote to football in poor countries reach their destination (see, for example, Hughes 2013; and Collette, Schulz, and Herzenberg 2010).

Most INGOs are free of the grosser sorts of corruption, but even the most philanthropic are not wholly able to deliver their funds to the intended beneficiaries. Many development INGOs maintain country offices that sub-contract work to local organizations and there are many more local NGOs than international. Workers in local NGOs need to earn a living and often require payment for attending meetings; controlling the costs of administration and staffing is not easy. Action Aid International, with a portfolio of activities not dissimilar to Oxfam, currently claims partnerships with more than two thousand locally based NGOs. The organization Plan estimates that it reaches 27 million children and their families in more than sixty thousand locations.

Not all NGOs are concerned with development. The environmental charity Greenpeace, founded in 1971 to protest against US nuclear testing in the Pacific, is more concerned with lobbying and direct action. Sea Shepherd, inclining even more towards direct action, operates anti-whaling vessels equipped with helicopters and drones to locate whaling fleets, which are then confronted. The organization has also mounted legal challenges against Californian restaurants serving whale meat. Human Rights Watch and Amnesty are concerned with justice, rather than economic development or environmental protection.

A second division among INGOs, often disregarded, is between those designed to be profitable and those that are not. Very often the term INGO is assumed to exclude the former and apply only to the latter. But firms with production facilities or the equivalent in more than one country under co-ordinated management are, in effect, international NGOs. To call them this is to signal that, while their primary objective may be profit, their economic activities have social and political consequences for which they bear responsibility, while their profitability depends, in large measure, on the ability of states to deliver security, an educated workforce, and effective infrastructure. It is important to recognize the importance of transnational corporations (TNCs) in the global system, alongside states, IGOs, and non-profit INGOs. To do otherwise is to fall into the trap of thinking of states as political and firms as economic, when both are clearly organizations that deploy material resources for the benefit – in theory at least – of publics and shareholders respectively.

A common feature of IR textbooks, bearing witness to the artificiality of the conventional division between economy and polity, is a table placing the national incomes of states and the revenues of leading transnational corporations (TNCs) together in rank order. Quite what juxtaposing BP, Exxon, General Motors, or Shell against Indonesia, South Africa, or Turkey is meant to prove is seldom clear. If it is that large companies are powerful, then this method understates the case. What ought to be compared with the revenue of a corporation is the revenue of a state, not the GNP of the country it governs. Like corporations, states are social agents; national economies are not. A state or a firm can be held responsible for its actions in a way that an entire nation cannot. This said, even the largest TNCs today have no armies. Gangs of superannuated marines hired to protect vulnerable facilities or scare Indigenous people off resource-rich land hardly compare to the East India Company armies that had conquered a third of India by the end of the eighteenth century. No modern corporation has come close to Stalin's Russia, Hitler's Germany, or Pol Pot's Cambodia in the level of atrocities committed. Nor can modern corporations readily call upon their parent states to bully other states on their behalf, always assuming that parentage is clear, which is often not the case. For the most part they are content with a division of labour by which the states in which they operate provide labour, infrastructure, a framework of law, and access to resources and markets for which they, in return, pay as little as they can get away with in wages, taxes, and royalties.

Set aside for a moment the terms of these bargains between state and firm, which have often come to appear grossly unfair with the passage of time. Set aside also the good faith of both parties, which has not always been assured. What remains is a moving frontier separating those activities thought appropriate for private exploitation and those thought inappropriate, either because they ought not to be a source of profit at all or because of their strategic importance. An important example in the former category is banking, often condemned in the past as usurious or exploitative by the Catholic Church. In its place the Church provided micro-lending facilities more consistent with its doctrines in many European and Latin American cities in the early modern period through the *montes de piedad* (mounts of piety). The merchant bankers of Europe happily ignored this sphere of relatively small-scale credit. From these firms, in the course of the nineteenth century, global networks of commercial banks, investment banks, and insurance companies emerged with their own sets of implicit norms about the propriety of different classes of transaction.

The desire of states to control money supply, to borrow on local money markets, and to control exchange rates led in time to the creation of central banks, to regulation of the private sector, and even to state acquisition of the entire banking sector in some countries. This process has been reversed more recently – a trend rudely interrupted following the 2008 financial crisis. The essentially liberal norms of orthodox global banking have also been challenged by Islamic banks and the Islamic 'windows' of conventional banks, based on different assumptions about the proper management of risk.

The two processes operating in the constant adjustment of relations between state and firm are norm-creation and change in the contours of the state. Norm-creation is the process by which certain forms of behaviour or social arrangements come to seem natural or unquestionable. Norms change. Two hundred years ago slavery was more common than it is today and far less widely condemned. It has certainly not disappeared. Estimates vary widely, principally because of difficulties of definition, but there are thought to be more slaves in the world today than at any previous time. Grouping various forms of debt bondage and forced labour together with internationally trafficked sex-workers, the total number of slaves may be as high as thirty million, though official estimates are lower. Yet today's slaves are a smaller percentage of the total world population than ever before. A marked normative change took place during the nineteenth century, prompted by sustained campaigning by abolitionist societies that would be called NGOs today. This led to emancipation throughout the British Empire (1833), in the USA (1863), in Russia (1861), and in Brazil (1888). Banking, too, has experienced marked changes in public opinion. Over the past two hundred years bankers have been seen successively as gamblers, exemplary professionals, and rapacious scoundrels. Once people feel the need to conceal, dissemble, or apologize for actions that would once have passed without comment, you know there's been a norm change.

A second aspect of the recent banking crisis has been adjustment of the frontier between the state and private sector. In the USA and Britain major financial institutions have been taken into public ownership. But it has generally been assumed that this is a temporary measure, because the frontier between public and private spheres has been moving steadily towards a more limited or reconfigured state, worldwide, over the past thirty years. State ownership of postal services, of transport systems such as railways or roads, and of public utilities has diminished as waves of privatization have swept across the world since 1980. The rise of private military contractors and security firms is part of this. Intermediate sectors, always private in some countries but jealously guarded by the state in others, have also seen an influx of private capital. These include broadcasting, the provision of health services, and the production of advanced-technology items with military applications.

IR, as it has been defined in this chapter, encompasses the transformation of global norms and the shifting frontier between state and private sectors. They can be regarded not simply as changes in the configuration of international society (the society of states) but of world society (the society of peoples). Changes in public–private distribution of welfare provision are not peripheral to IR, but central. This is because the balance of power between states that lies at the heart of the most conservative characterizations of international relations depends in the last resort on the ability of states to mobilize the resources required to ensure national security. States that rely largely on INGOs and their local partners or transnational firms to deliver health and education, or depend on workers born elsewhere for the operation of key sectors, cannot expect to command the unconditional loyalty of the public that is needed to wage a sustained conventional war. The functionalists were partly right. Open economies cannot be sustained during prolonged conflicts without sacrifices that depend on just that unqualified loyalty. Wars can still be fought, but they increasingly depend either on professional volunteer forces or irregular forces that sustain themselves by plunder.

Dispersal of what were once thought essential functions of the state across a spectrum of organizations – private and public, local and international – has changed the nature of armed conflict. The multitude of INGOs operating in the Global South, the three or four hundred leading TNCs, and the large numbers of migrant workers, at every level of skill and remuneration, living outside their birth countries, together put in question the capability of states to engage in mass mobilization. At the same time they expand the agenda of IR beyond relations between states to embrace trade, investment, and migration. Bundled together, these developments are captured in a single word: globalization.

Globalization and the Widening IR Agenda

The great expansion of trade, international investment, and migration that took place in the later nineteenth century has come to be referred to as the first globalization. This process was already faltering before 1914, and was subsequently halted and then reversed. 'Globalization' is a term coined to describe the post-1945 recovery in international trade, investment, and migration that was starting to exceed pre-1914 levels by the 1980s. The term rose from a very low frequency of usage during the 1980s, overtaking 'internationalization' around 1993. The underlying argument of those who adopted the term was that transnational market forces had become so strong that it was no longer possible for national economic management to control them. Territorially defined states were rapidly losing power. Conversely, TNCs were gaining power through their ability to co-ordinate research, production, and sales heedless of state frontiers. Globalization consisted in a step-change in the volume of international transactions coupled with a tendency towards cultural uniformity.

Sceptics pointed out that international transactions had, if anything, been higher before 1914 than in the 1980s relative to those within national economies, and that most large corporations depended on a strong base in a single country. One significant measure of global economic integration is the ratio of merchandise trade (imports plus exports) to GDP. For France, Japan, the UK, and the USA this was lower in 1973 than it had been in 1913; for Germany it was only marginally higher. Even the sceptics admitted, however, that the world economy was exhibiting some new features in the 1990s. Chief among these was an unprecedented volume of trade in currencies and securities. Comparisons were often made between recent years and the late nineteenth century, and it is likely that completion of a global network of telegraphic communication in the 1870s was decisive in effecting a fundamental transformation, similar to that facilitated by computers and mobile phones in the more recent period.

Improved communications allowed materials and components to move along the value-added chain more rapidly and predictably. During the first globalization this allowed firms to operate with greatly reduced stocks. This in turn released large sums for investment in the capital-intensive industries of the so-called 'Second Industrial Revolution', such as electricity generation, oil, and automobiles. Since the 1990s developments in information technology have yielded similar productivity gains, facilitating the rise of newly industrialized countries (NICs) including Brazil, China, and India. Recent economic growth, especially outside the established industrial economies bordering the North Atlantic, has been on such a scale that few sceptics remain. The second globalization is unquestioned, and even the post-2008 crisis in North America and Western Europe has not reversed it. Global trade and foreign direct investment have risen significantly and the reliance of major corporations on a 'home' country has diminished. These trans-border flows have been joined by migration at levels approaching those of the nineteenth century.

Migration

Though current migration figures look high, contemporary movement of peoples appears insignificant in proportion to total global population, hardly matching the wholesale movements of Germanic tribes into Europe in the twilight of the Western Roman Empire or the massive migrations from Europe into temperate America and Australasia from the mid-nineteenth century. At the end of 2008 there were fifteen million people officially classified as refugees worldwide. This is a deplorable index of human misery, but at 0.2% of global population it is *relatively* small. Victims of forced labour were estimated at 12.3 million, a not dissimilar number. Students attending universities outside their home countries, numbering 3.3 million in 2009, were even fewer, though their membership of global elites makes them a force to contend with in the future and should caution host states to treat them better. The number of economic migrants is harder to measure, but the money they send home to their dependants is a fair proxy, since it captures enduring links with a country of origin, eliminating many of those who – though foreign born – have settled permanently in a new country. These remittances amount to less than one percent of global income. Average net migration into the more developed regions of the world, meanwhile, was running at just 2.2 per thousand of the recipient population between 2005 and 2010.

These aggregate figures obscure the very marked impact of cross-frontier migration, free and forced, on particular countries. In 2008 almost half the world's refugees were living in states bordering Israel, the human residue of decades of unresolved Arab–Israeli conflict. At the time of writing, fresh concentrations of refugees were accumulating nearby on the borders of war-torn Syria. In March 2013 it was estimated that as many as a million Syrians had fled the country. Two years before, large numbers had been fleeing from drought and conflict in the Horn of Africa and Libya. The first of these caused severe problems in Kenya. There, Dadaab refugee camp rapidly became the largest in the world with a peak population of half a million, while a spate of grenade attacks by Somalis thought to belong to the militant Islamist al-Shabaab group led the Kenyan government to clear refugees from urban areas, late in 2012, by withdrawing aid supplies. Coupled with greater security at home, this Kenyan pressure had led to some Somalis returning home by the start of 2013, but many still remained. The second flow triggered civil war in Mali, provoked by the return of migrant mercenaries from Libya, prompting French intervention in 2013. The tsunami of 2004 and the Haitian earthquake of 2010 produced similar crises. If the United Nations High Commission for Refugees (UNHCR) together with national aid agencies and NGOs do their job, these additions to the refugee population will be temporary. But like the permanent refugee population, they are spatially concentrated.

Forced labour has lately been predominantly an Asian problem (seventy-seven percent of all victims) though disproportionately lucrative for criminals in Europe and the USA, where half the estimated \$32 billion annual profits accrue. At the close of the first decade of the new century seventy percent of international university students were located in just eight countries, almost half of them in four leading anglophone destinations: the USA (twenty percent), the UK (thirteen percent), Australia (seven percent), and Canada (four percent). Remittances were also concentrated, constituting a significant source of income for countries that have specialized in the export of labour, such as Guyana (where they amount to twenty-six percent of GNP), Honduras (twenty-two percent), or the Philippines (eleven percent), though there is no such reliance in more populous countries with relatively high absolute levels of remittances such as Mexico (three percent) or China (one percent). Conversely, remittances from the USA, at close to $3 billion in 2007, were insignificant in relation to the size of the US economy, which at $63 trillion still accounted for almost a quarter of world output.

Finally, net inward migration, the cause of so much anxiety in many recipient countries, is very unevenly distributed, concentrated in specific countries and, within them, in particular regions, cities, and neighbourhoods. The USA has traditionally been a country of refuge and settlement. In consequence, the number of non-natives entering the country since 1990, at a little short of 22 million, is nothing out of the ordinary, amounting to about seven percent of total population, many of whom will by now have been naturalized. At 3.3 per thousand, net annual recorded migration to the USA between 2005 and 2010 was well below nineteenth-century rates, which reached 14 per thousand in mid-century and rose again to 10 per thousand (of a much larger aggregate population) between 1900 and 1914. It is not absolute numbers that have made cross-frontier population movement in all its varied forms a matter of recent concern, but its uneven distribution, experienced directly by some and observed through the mass media by many more. Added to this is a widespread fear that social and cultural integration may now happen less readily than in the past, because of the relative ease with which contact with the country of origin can be sustained, and home culture transplanted to new soil. This fear is a political asset for the extreme Right in Europe and the USA.

Population movement is the aspect of globalization that shows the least advance on nineteenth-century levels quantitatively, yet poses some of the greatest social and political challenges. In so doing, it sets an agenda that goes beyond international politics

(IP), as traditionally conceived. On the one hand it has mobilized transnational criminal enterprises, banks greedy for commissions on remittances, and great armies of national bureaucrats, whose business it is to record and regulate flows of economic migrants and asylum seekers in response to nativist concerns. On the other hand it has created unprecedented possibilities to sustain relationships, extended across thousands of miles, through the use of mobile phones and the internet. Services such as Skype and Facebook do not obliterate distance, but they make the creation and persistence of cross-border imagined communities very much easier than ever before. Furthermore, this ability to live in two worlds has made it possible to resist the traditional preferences of host states for integration or multiculturalism; complex hybrid identities can be developed instead.

Two concepts require development here: the hybridity referred to just now, and the imagined community. The latter term was coined by Benedict Anderson in 1983 when defining the nation. True communities – a village or a school, for example – are developed by constant proximity, direct acquaintance, and repeated social interaction between their members. The cultivation of imagined national communities, whose members might never meet and could certainly not assemble to take decisions, had been a powerful device of modern states, fostered by military conscription, national sporting contests, anthems, state broadcasting services, and the like. Once, only states and organized religions could hope to create communities of this sort and mobilize the loyalties of their members. The low cost and sophistication of new information technologies has meant that the ability to generate imagined communities is now very much more widespread. Sub-cultures based on shared interests as diverse as tango, wildlife conservation, and military re-enactment are able to organize globally. With the profusion of imagined communities comes a step-change in the political economy of loyalty. Where once loyalties might be pictured as a set of concentric circles: family, village, province, nation, and beyond, they now appear, for many, to be a more complex array, varying in relative intensity over time and lacking clear hierarchical or spatial structure.

Integration of migrants into a new country once consisted in the abandonment of one imagined community and the adoption of another. More recently, multiculturalism has been based on the idea of the coexistence of communities with differing cultural loyalties within a single polity. Some Indians who have settled in Britain, for example, continue to support the Indian cricket team in matches against their adopted country. Hybridity has been used to describe a novel consciousness in which identities do not so much compete or coexist as interact, with rapid switching between or simultaneous performance of a multiplicity of roles.

What's in a Name? – International Politics, Relations, Affairs, and Studies

The organizations, institutions, and processes that have been described so far have attracted the attention of scholars and generated a huge demand for university courses. Across many countries people pretty much know what they mean by economics or physics or maths. But university departments, journals, and programmes of study in the field explored here have a variety of names: International Politics, International Relations, International Affairs, and International Studies. There is not much consistency in the use of these terms but, very roughly, International Politics suggests a sub-field of the discipline of Political Science, International Relations (IR) makes a claim for equal status with other, more established social sciences, International Affairs signals close concern with contemporary policy-making, and International Studies implies the practical application of several existing disciplines – usually including law, history, economics, political science, and sociology – to a distinctive set of problems. Throw in postgraduate programmes with fancy titles such as War Studies, Peace Studies, Public Affairs, or Diplomacy, and the newcomer may be forgiven for serious confusion. There is little consistency in the use of these terms. The approach of Jacques Thomassen and his Dutch colleagues, by which students had to study each component discipline in their programme on its own terms, might better be referred to as International Studies; but they insisted on calling it Political Science, unwilling to surrender that title to US academics without a fight.

Not long ago a mathematician nearing the end of his first degree consulted one of his teachers about what to do next. He was considering a master's in Economics or International Relations. His adviser, also a mathematician, thought for a moment before observing that the trouble with people in International Relations was that they were all really historians, really lawyers, or ... really stupid. This waspish little story helps explain why the profusion of names has persisted. Disciplines form and reform over time, but innovation has to be justified. This generally requires the development of a comprehensive theory or a distinctive method of inquiry. The economy is not a natural thing; it is conjured up by selecting, from a complex universe of social interactions, the sub-set that best lends itself to a particular method of inquiry based on restrictive assumptions about rational behaviour. International Relations has no such method and, as a new field of study, has remained preoccupied for several decades with the development of a coherent discipline and a recognized academic brand.

Scholars recognize this, some regarding it as a shortcoming to be overcome, others resisting such strict disciplinarity. Those in each camp like to be precise. Their hair-splitting can easily become pedantic. Yet these wrangles about naming are justified. Extreme abstraction can reduce the international system to its bare bones: a multiplicity of states under no supreme authority, among which relations are largely dictated by relative power. There is no denying that the simplicity of such an approach generates a productive research agenda and some profound insights. Yet some of the most important transformations wrought by globalization are private and intangible, affecting personal and collective identities and related loyalties – such as nationality, ideology, and religion – that motivate political action, but taking place beyond the reach of the state. Whereas the relatively hard social sciences of economics, politics, and sociology strive to explain complex patterns of global causality, a vital place remains for history, anthropology, and cultural studies if migration, cross-frontier and inter-communal violence, and the inequalities to which they give rise, are to be fully understood. This is the start of an answer to the question of why the broad agenda and disciplinary eclecticism of IR, as sketched in this chapter, has the edge over the more restricted approach of International Politics.

Even among those who regard it as a separate discipline, scholarly inquiry into relations between nations has no unique method. It borrows here and there to supplement the basic understanding of an anarchic system. Meanwhile, universities need to organize their staff and students into faculties, publishers need to sort their lists by subject, scholars need to exchange ideas with their peers at the conferences of professional associations, and faculties annually turn out new cohorts of professionals branded with their name: no longer lawyers, economists, or historians with interests in international affairs, but IR scholars. (There is, significantly, no neat term to describe them, equivalent to historian, lawyer, or economist.) In this way IR has developed as the institutional form of a discipline despite its lack of methodological unity or an agreed technical vocabulary.

A second truth underlying that 'really stupid' quip has to do with subject matter. Method helps define many academic disciplines. Social anthropologists are defined by ethnography, the detailed description of a community in its own terms based on a sustained period living within it. But many disciplines are defined as much by their characteristic object of inquiry as by method. Among the social sciences, economics, history, and politics developed as separate disciplines around the same time that the nation-state reached its peak of development in Europe and North America. The objective of nationalism was to align people, territory, statehood, and – ideally – language as closely as possible. Their precise coincidence in the so-called nation-state was its seldom-achieved ideal. One indication that the trick was working was the unquestioning devotion of academic historians to the history of the nation-state or of lawyers to the legal system of a single country. Economics not only abstracts certain kinds of behaviour but also, in the study of macroeconomics, chooses to examine the workings of a bounded national economy. This was made easier by the creation of national statistical offices and other institutions that made possible consistent measurement within a single country. Even today cross-frontier economic transactions are typically relegated to the final chapter in introductory texts on macroeconomics. Not very long ago, few lawyers accepted international law as proper law.

So IR turns out not only to be a disputable name for a field of study with no agreed approach, feeding off the leavings of its elder siblings. It is the runt of the social science litter. Yet this is precisely why IR has such tremendous critical edge. Switching metaphors, it can be thought of as an acid, eating into cracks in the apparently solid edifice of the nation-based disciplines, etching the lines of cross-frontier transactions between individuals and organizations to reveal unsuspected patterns. At the same time, it considers global society systemically, as something more than the sum of those transactions. First tempted in by concern about the plight of the world, the student is likely to be retained by the intellectual challenge of a project that has been strongly critical from the outset, working against the grain of common sense and vested interest – in effect an anti-discipline.

What had it best be called, this anti-discipline? In both the United States and Britain, the leading professional bodies retain 'Studies' in their titles: The International Studies Association (ISA), the British International Studies Association (BISA), and the more recent World International Studies Committee (WISC) have all chosen this path as the most inclusive option. 'Studies' does nothing to prevent those who identify as political scientists or IR scholars from joining, yet sociologists and lawyers do not have to jump ship to take part. But this is a shade nostalgic. The naming of those associations was done for reasons that were valid a generation ago, when a majority of those teaching the subject had backgrounds in other disciplines. Today, the best compromise is 'International Relations'. IR acknowledges the *de facto* separation from other social sciences without compromising the eclecticism that is, for so many, the principal source of innovation and excitement in the field. Fortunately this conforms to the tendency of current usage on both sides of the Atlantic. 'International Relations' became the preferred term at the end of the 1980s as 'International Affairs', with its suggestion of close proximity to policy-makers, faded away after a period of mid-century dominance. 'International Studies' comes in an honourable second. Figure 1 (opposite) shows the relative frequency of these terms in British and US English in graphic form.

IR characteristically divides generalizations about international relations into two rough camps: realist and liberal. Realists are said to emphasize the centrality of states and the inevitability of conflict between them, to be settled by rational pursuit of national interest through the exercise of power. They are generally pessimistic about the possibility that international co-operation or law can ultimately substitute for more coercive means of conflict resolution. For this reason they generally dismiss the possibility of progress in human affairs or improvement of human nature. Liberal internationalists, idealists, or utopianists,

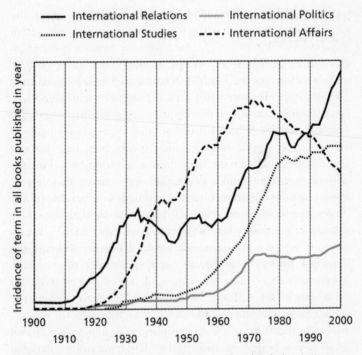

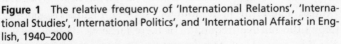

Figure 1 The relative frequency of 'International Relations', 'International Studies', 'International Politics', and 'International Affairs' in English, 1940–2000
Source: Google nGrams (US and British English).

generally referred to as liberals in this book (never liberalists!), are presented as altogether more optimistic, believing that peaceful resolution of conflicts is possible. They hold that common interests on which to base conflict resolution are out there in the world, waiting to be found. Social engineering – in the form of enlightened regulation, economic management, and international organization – can disclose those shared interests, even when they have long been obscured by privilege, misinformation, or misunderstanding.

International Politics v. International Relations

To confirm the usefulness of IR and catch a first glimpse of its leading theoretical traditions, it is worth turning briefly to two very different realist attempts to set limits to international politics, the first by taxonomy and the second – very much more briefly – by theory. Taxonomy is the classification or arrangement of subject matter. The division of living things by class, order, family, genus, and species lies at the heart of zoology. The periodic table of chemical elements is a taxonomy, showing a systematic arrangement of elements. It stimulated inquiry by predicting the existence and characteristics of elements as yet undiscovered. Theory, by contrast, seeks to impose an explanation on a set of observed regularities and offers conditional predictions of the form 'if x, then y' that can be tested against events or in the laboratory.

What is the subject matter of IR? What makes up international relations? One frequently repeated definition derives from Hedley Bull, an Australian who taught at Oxford in the mid-twentieth century. Bull is chosen because he has had a profound influence on the so-called International Society or English School approach to international relations, which offers a middle way between realism and liberalism. He quite deliberately restricted his attention to international politics. He was a realist in his concentration on relations between states, and leaned towards liberalism in his belief that order and justice could be achieved through the operation of institutions. By institutions he did not mean organizations, but patterns of behaviour regulated by custom and norms. In *The Anarchical Society*, his most widely read book, Bull distinguished five institutions that, together, constituted international society, or the society of states. These were the balance of power, international law and organization, diplomacy, war, and Great Power management. In their characteristic modern forms these institutions originated in Europe and then spread throughout the world. At best, states participated in them with the intention of securing a balance between order and justice. The patterns of interaction between states facilitated by them were what constituted international politics.

This taxonomy is as interesting for what it leaves out as for what it includes. Where are trade and migration? Where are the world's great religions? Where are the people? Any wider understanding of international relations would be bound to include them. Nor can restriction of the scope of inquiry to international *politics* really exclude them, for they figure prominently in the calculations of states. So what justifies setting the limits just so?

There are three things to be said about this. The first is that the nation is something larger than and distinct from the state; so it seems odd to confine the inter-*national* politics of Bull's title to relations between states. 'International' promises more than the study of statecraft. The second point is that Bull's states were historically specific. Suppose IR were to concern itself only with them, and not with relations between other kinds of political organization, past and future. It might then be a useful and pragmatic *training* for intending policy-makers but could hardly claim to be a social *science* generating taxonomies and theories that apply universally. It would be as though zoology had decided to limit itself to human physiology: an entirely justifiable decision on pragmatic grounds, since it is studied exclusively by humans, but one with considerable intellectual costs.

In common speech the words 'country', 'nation', and 'state' are often interchangeable. But they refer to three quite distinct things: a defined territory, the people who live there (or believe they have a right to), and the ultimate legal and military authority in that territory. Some countries are bounded by so-called natural frontiers such as oceans, mountain ranges, marshlands, or wide rivers. Others are not. Still others manage to operate successfully in spite of physical obstacles that might be thought insurmountable. Canada and the United States only overcame the obstacles presented by mountain ranges through heroic engineering and after much human suffering. Yet many take for granted the division of Argentina from Chile by the high Andes, forgetting that indigenous polities of the region straddled the southern reaches of this *cordillera* without too much difficulty before their final conquest by the European intruders in the nineteenth century, while several provinces east of the *cordillera*, now in Argentina, were ruled from Santiago de Chile in colonial times.

The attempt to align nation and state has already been noted. Some states comprise several nations, each distinguished from its neighbours by history and language, often with an element of political autonomy. It follows that there are nations lacking their own state. The cumbersomely named United Kingdom of Great Britain and Northern Ireland includes Welsh, Scots, and Irish populations as well as English (though hardly the whole of any of these, given that the number of Britons living permanently outside the UK was estimated at 5.5 million by the BBC in 2012). Canada was formed in 1867 by a fusion of British and French colonies; Spain is an uneasy amalgam of several distinct language communities: Basque, Galician, Catalan, and Castilian. In each of these countries many people are content with current arrangements, but in every case there is an element of dissent. Significant elements among the Scots, Basques, Quebecers, and Catalans aspire to align nation and state. Some still hanker after a united Ireland.

Bull's definition attempts to close off some of the space created by distinguishing between country, nation, and state. To reduce international relations to the dealings of states is commonplace, but it has strongly restrictive implications for what IR ought properly to be concerned with. There are plenty of countries that are home to more than one nation or political community, for which a single state provides security and government. Spain and

South Africa are obvious examples. It would follow that a literal understanding of inter-*national* relations might still reasonably include relations between the component *nations* – as between Scotland and England – though not necessarily those of one *state* with another. It would surely also include private foreign commerce and overseas investment, migration, and colonization by the nationals of the country concerned, and the influence arising from the diffusion of aspects of national cultures, such as literature, music, religion, or law (which often owes as much to custom as to the command of any sovereign).

Is it of concern to IR that Bostonians of Irish descent used to fund IRA fighters against the British? Should IR scholars care that Welsh speakers from southern Argentina still compete in cultural festivals or Eisteddfods in Wales, more than a century after emigrating? Is it of interest to IR that some mosques in Bradford or Detroit come under attack from Christian zealots or preach a violent form of Jihad? The answer to each of these questions is yes, though the salience of the issues varies. It follows that IR should concern itself with the sociology of diasporas, the institutional residue of collapsed empires and states, and aspects of global culture, as well as with the declared interests and objectives of state policy-makers and diplomats. All these subjects have become concerns of modern states and preoccupations of IR scholars in the course of a great blossoming of global society that was already under way at the time Bull was writing.

If marginalization of the nation distinguishes Bull's International Politics from a more inclusive International Relations, a second remarkable feature of his formulation is that it assumes the core business of IR to be the interpretation of relations among a very particular group of polities. It's not just about states: it's about modern states. But the modern state is not the only form of supreme or sovereign political authority. It is distinguished by its profoundly bureaucratic character and its aspiration to align state and nation in the nation-state. In the past there have been tribes, tyrannies, city-states, theocracies, and multinational empires galore. Reach back to the early modern period and Europe was a patchwork of empires, kingdoms, principalities, bishoprics, and republics, regulated by the fluctuating fortunes of dynasties such as the Habsburgs, the Bourbons, or the Tudors, and by the vagaries of intermarriage and inheritance. Statecraft was a dangerous profession that could end in loss of life and property at the whim of a monarch. So it has remained, except in those states where bureaucracy and the rule of law have tempered military prowess and hereditary authority. Reach back only a century or so and consider the profusion of nationalities, languages, and creeds within the Austro-Hungarian, Tsarist, Ottoman, or Chinese empires. Reach out across the world today and the aspirations of the modern state are seldom attained. How many of them can boast of complete control over their territories, effective administrative systems reaching to the smallest settlements, consistent application of the law, and universal loyalty? How many Indigenous peoples tolerate the pretensions of a distant state while quietly and stubbornly upholding their own customs?

Rather than treating it as a model, it is better to regard the modern state as one variety of a more general type of entity, defined by its unwillingness to acknowledge superior authority. The genus or class is political community or polity; the modern state is one species within the genus. Its varieties include democracies, tyrannies, kleptocracies, and plain failures. Nor should those fortunate enough to live in democracies feel smug about it. Writing of the rule of law, Guillermo O'Donnell, the foremost Argentine political scientist of his generation, had good reason – given the troubled history of his country – to remind his readers that his subject was not democracy, but processes of 'endless and always potentially reversible democratization'. As voting and party membership decline, those in so-called mature democracies should take note.

In short, both the entities and the institutions that constituted international society for Bull are subject to change over time. The entities – Bull's modern states – did not always exist and may in time be superseded by new political forms; indeed there are those who claim that this is already happening. Furthermore, Bull's preferred institutions, such as international law or the balance of power, are specific to relations between modern states, and are most characteristic of a single set of these entities, the North Atlantic states of his own day.

It might seem a small step from Europe to Latin America, where states ruled by people of European descent won independence early in the nineteenth century. Here were modern polities patterned on European states, yet which seldom fought wars. Their most intense external relations in the late nineteenth and early twentieth centuries were not with one another, as in Europe, but with transnational business corporations and bankers from Europe and North America, and with the parent states of those firms. Their calendar of international relations is punctuated by economic crises, not the outbreak or conclusion of wars: 1825, 1873, 1890, 1929, and 1982 figure more prominently than 1870, 1914–18, or 1939–45. These American states developed a different blend of Bull's institutions in their mutual relations, with greater emphasis on law and international organization and less on war. Since all bar Brazil shared Spanish as a common language, political exile was much easier than in multilingual Europe, making possible the development of a supranational elite culture and solidarity that came to serve as an additional institution of international society.

The characteristic Western-hemisphere emphasis on international economic relations has already been noted, and was evident in the primacy of trade, investment, and migration in relations between the Old World and the New during the nineteenth century. More subtly, it helps explain the United States' reluctance to protect its global economic interests by permanent rule over overseas territories of the sort favoured in the past by Europeans, and the very modest scale of United States armed forces up to 1917. For Europeans the modern distinction between war and trade was slow to develop, war being as much a means of enrichment as a tool of statecraft, while markets for commodities and labour were characterized as much by coercion as by free and fair exchange. By the time the USA rose to global pre-eminence, a clearer separation of economic relations from politics had developed in relations between the Great Powers, and it was only after its intervention in the initially European First World War that the USA reluctantly began to militarize.

Meanwhile, in small wars on the American frontiers, north and south, a growing body of ethno-history shows the distinctions between war, diplomacy, and trade have remained blurred. To allow that late nineteenth-century relations between Washington and the Plains Indians are just as legitimate a topic for IR as contemporaneous Franco-German rivalry over Alsace and Lorraine is also to admit variability in the institutions of international society.

The broader relations of nation with nation, the collective response of states to shared predicaments such as epidemic disease or global warming, and the interactions of lesser polities: these are all very well. But a realist might reply that the fundamental condition of these social relations and forms of political co-operation has always been, and is bound to remain, the ability of the world's most powerful polities to maintain a stable states-system. In this story the interactions of NGOs and lesser states are both regarded as subordinate. The American Civil War (1861–65) and the 1885 revolt of Sudanese leader Mohammad Ahmed (1844–85), self-proclaimed Madhi, against Egyptian rule may plausibly be characterized as unintended consequences of central European geopolitical rivalries: mere sub-plots. As the USA and Egypt shaped up to play their intended parts in the Great Power game, weaknesses in their internal constitutions were exposed. So the Soviet Union discovered as it tried to tackle Afghanistan in the 1980s, precipitating the end of the Cold War. Global trade and investment matter to those directly concerned, but their larger political significance lies in their contribution to the tax base and military competence of the state. For the realist it's always the big story that matters. Without security nothing else can be achieved, and global security depends on relations between the major powers in which the transformation of national capabilities into military power is ultimately decisive.

Second, while polities may vary over time, there is one distinctive feature that all sovereign entities possess, and that is ultimate responsibility for their own survival. Kenneth Waltz, probably the most influential single theorist of international relations in the USA over the past forty years, wrote of them as self-help units operating under anarchy, a word which here does not mean disorder but simply the absence of any higher authority. In his vision, the greater part of the behaviour of states was conditioned by the anarchic structure of the international system and the distribution of capabilities across it. A state that ignores systemic pressures will not survive any more than a firm that persistently ignores market signals. The extreme abstraction of this model allowed for theorizing about the relative stability of systems of states across time and space in which the only significant variable was polarity (bi-, multi-, or uni-) or, in less formal terms, the balance of power. This, Waltz argued, was more likely to prove stable if bipolar than multipolar. Systemic pressures dominate, and all else is detail.

Together, these two objections might seem to restore the primacy of states as the typical actors in international relations, and of diplomacy, international law, international organization, balancing, and war as regulators of the system. But in his sparse *Theory of International Politics* Waltz inadvertently let the broader agenda in again by the back door. What's in play as the world's Great Powers confront one another is not simply military might or 'hard' power, to borrow a phrase from Joseph Nye, another leading US scholar and government adviser. It consists in the combined capabilities of each state, which turn out to include their national economies. But in democracies these lie beyond the formal control of the state, as do Nye's 'soft power' resources, such as culture, higher education systems, or political ideals. So the nation reappears and the agenda of IP once again widens to conform to that of IR.

Hedley Bull and Kenneth Waltz advocated a narrow agenda centring on the core concerns of leading states and on conflict between states and its resolution. For them, this ineradicable conflict set the terms on which other kinds of interactions between the world's nations took place. This made them influential representatives of the realist school. But Bull never explicitly justified his exclusion of economic and social interactions while Waltz, for his part, reintroduced them into the play of power through his encompassing definition of capabilities.

The preference for a broad view of the content of international relations and the appropriate objects of study for IR has often coincided with liberal understandings of conflict between states and its resolution. A principal reason for this is the liberal belief that international commerce, international organization, and democracy act as pacific influences, creating interests inimical to war and constraining the belligerent tendencies of states.

The provisional conclusion must be that both realists and liberals offer good reason to doubt the view that international relations should concern itself solely with the state and its security. Indeed, Security Studies, as a sub-field of IR, has long since widened its scope to include non-state threats to security, such as natural disaster and environmental pollution, while also extending the range of objects of security to include peoples as well as states. Human security has, for many, displaced state security, and the difference is as much one of agenda as of attitude.

Stereotypes of Realism and Liberalism

Realism:
- The state is the central actor in international politics.
- It is sovereign, acknowledging no superior authority.
- The system of states is anarchic.
- This structure conditions and dominates the intentions of actors within it.
- Its character is determined by the distribution of power across it.
- Each state must rely in the last resort on its own resources to survive.
- The interests of states in a world of scarce resources are necessarily conflictual.
- Other states can never be wholly trusted.
- The prudence of military preparedness outweighs the risk of provocation.
- Co-operation with other states is never easy.
- Progress is illusory.

Liberalism:
- Political community is the source of legitimate political authority and sovereignty.
- States are the agents of nations or peoples.
- Together they constitute a society of states governed by norms and institutions.
- States have common interests.
- It is possible to establish trust and achieve co-operation.
- Enduring progress is possible.

There are die-hards on both sides. They include those who continue to insist on the centrality of states and those who see states as villains or think them increasingly irrelevant. Back in 1977 Robert Keohane and Joseph Nye suggested a face-saving compromise in an influential book about global co-operation: we can look at the world either as the play of state power, in which co-operation is regulated by states with relative advantage in mind, or as a space in which co-operation creates webs of interdependence, limiting or reconfiguring the power of states. Which interpretation is the more appropriate guide to action at any point in time is a matter of judgement. By claiming that these views of the world were better thought of as interpretations, rather than descriptions, Keohane and Nye damaged those claims for the scientific status of IR that depended on the possibility of a unique, value-free description for any specific set of events. But they decisively opened up the field by reminding policy-makers of the responsibility and judgement required when balancing considerations of power and morality, self-interest and altruism, the short- and the long-term view. Nor did they abandon the claim of IR to be a social science. Theory is not the sole hallmark of social scientific endeavour. Taxonomy, analysis, and interpretation may be less powerful and elegant, but are no less useful.

To adopt a narrow realist or political science approach to international relations would almost certainly result in IR departments in universities becoming estranged from their students, relatively few of whom set out to become politicians or servants of the state, let alone academics. To a great extent, the widening agenda of IR has reflected real changes in the scope of international relations and growth in the number and variety of those interested and engaged in them. The more liberal interpretation captured by the phrase international relations is not just wishful thinking. It reflects the world as it is, at least as realistically as political realism.

2
The shadow of history

The world is managed by men and women who generally have at least twenty-five years' personal memory of events and may also have been schooled in more remote history. Past events provide a vocabulary for thinking about current problems. They do not offer ready-made solutions, and to think that they can is dangerous. Generals have been notoriously prone to fight the last war, and lose it. Learning from years of static trench warfare on the Western Front during the First World War, the French spent three billion francs building impregnable fixed defensive positions during the 1930s. In 1940 German forces simply outflanked this Maginot Line by invading France through neutral Belgium. Harking back to this and other errors, Barack Obama warned in his 2008 presidential campaign that the USA was in danger of 'constantly fighting the last war, responding to the threats that have come to fruition, instead of staying one step ahead of the threats of the 21st century'.

This said, knowledge of history can help to situate current problems and explain how those on the other side of the table may be thinking, provided it is used with discretion. There *are* lessons from history, but it's hard to know which of them are to be trusted. There are also technical terms in history, defining different approaches to the subject, which have implications for the study of international relations. The most obvious of these is the distinction between modern and contemporary history. Modern history looks forward from a point in the past, often to justify the present; contemporary history looks back in search of guidance for current predicaments. That word 'modern' has been used repeatedly in this book. But what, precisely, does it mean? The short answer is, 'after 1453'; but unless you know what happened in 1453, and what it has meant to people since, this doesn't help very much. To get the hang of International Relations it helps to know a little history; to succeed as a practitioner of international relations it may be best to forget the history you know. The past really *is* a foreign country and they *did* do things differently there.

Academics used to believe that history began with writing. Only where written records and monumental inscriptions remained was there any chance of constructing a narrative of past events or critically evaluating accounts written at the time. The Greeks and the Romans wrote histories. Many of these survived the collapse of the ancient world and were passed on by their Arab and Byzantine guardians to modern Europe, where some familiarity with the Classics became, for several hundred years, a mark of gentility. More recently, archaeology and the decipherment of more scripts and languages extended knowledge of the ancient world. Yet history remained until recently the record of literate elites: written by and about kings, priests, nobility, generals, and their confidential advisers. International history was therefore confined to the study of past relations between sovereigns, largely reliant on state archives. This was realist history – centred on states and conflict.

Steeped in this tradition, Hugh Trevor-Roper, Regius Professor of Modern History at Oxford, notoriously declared in 1963 that Africa had no history. In a very narrow sense he was right: the written record was sparse. But already oral history and archaeological evidence were being used to chart the spread of Islam along the caravan routes of the Sahara to the Savannah belt and to recapture the rise and fall of pre-colonial African states and empires. History and social anthropology spawned ethno-history, vastly extending knowledge of the past and providing a parallel, within academic history, to the liberal interpretation of international relations. Meanwhile, in the wealthy states of the North, oral history and neglected written records were being used to challenge elite and masculine domination of national histories and often rode roughshod over the national and class frontiers those elites had fought so hard to establish.

Three examples give a sense of the new style of history. Among the most impressive, for sheer detective work, is Rebecca Scott's study of the Vinent/Tinchant family, which traces a 'creole trajectory' across three generations and numerous Atlantic crossings, to account for how a Fulani woman from West Africa, trafficked to the Caribbean, renamed Rosalie, and subsequently liberated in the Haitian revolution, came to be the grandmother of an Antwerp cigar manufacturer and politician. Her daughter, Elizabeth, born in Saint-Domingue in 1799, married Jacques Tinchant, a free man of colour, in 1822. They emigrated from New Orleans to France in 1840 to secure a better future for their children. There, Rosalie's grandson, Edouard Tinchant, was born in 1841. By the time he had grown up, the family had moved to Belgium, where his father established a cigar store and factory. This business took Edouard to New Orleans in 1861, where he fought for the Union in the Civil War and was a delegate to the Louisiana constitutional convention of 1867–68; he later returned to Belgium. Lives were not all lived within the frontiers of states. Mobility was less easy in those days, but far from impossible.

Patching together this story from scraps in a dozen archives, Scott's work is a particularly virtuosic example of the new transgressive history. But the exploration of global lives had begun a generation before. In the north Italian town of Prato, a merchant left his house to the municipality on his death in 1410. By chance the written records of his business survived in a cupboard and were rediscovered in 1870. From them Iris

Origo was able to trace a network of commercial and personal transactions stretching from Bruges to Fez and from London to Alexandria. Around the same time, the French historian Emmanuel Le Roy Ladurie was exploring the papers of Jacques Fournier (1280–1342). As bishop of Pamiers, in what is today the South of France, Fournier had vigorously opposed heresy. From interrogation transcripts of suspected heretics and witnesses, Le Roy Ladurie was able to reconstruct the migratory culture of fourteenth-century shepherds. These shepherds were heterodox in their religious beliefs and vague about their political loyalties; their communities straddled the southern Pyrenees. What was Spain or France to them? What was the Church (until it turned and bit them)? Written in the aftermath of the two world wars, what made these novel histories so important was their challenge to the prevailing nationalistic style of academic and schoolroom history. International history, they demonstrated, could be about more than dynasty, diplomacy, and war. It also embraced those who had worked against the grain of rising nationalism.

An Outline of World History

There is, in short, much more history than there used to be. To the history of empires and nations have now been added the histories of peoples and persons, all of which makes for a better fit between history and multidisciplinary IR, but also makes any summary more difficult. To get some sort of grip on it you need to take a step back.

Recorded history began with permanent settlement and agriculture, notably in the fertile lower valleys of the Nile, the Indus, the Yangtze, and Yellow Rivers, and Mesopotamia. Only large-scale agriculture produced surpluses of storable grain on a sufficient scale to support aristocracies and priesthoods and provide the labour needed for irrigation systems, conquest, temples, and palaces. Often, the political form of these civilizations was the tribute-empire, in which populations were taxed, or laid under tribute, by a dominant clan, dynasty, or priesthood. Migratory pastoralists operating as nations-in-arms or hordes were able to create extensive empires and may have done so since time immemorial, but they only entered the historical record when they ran up against sedentary peoples whose scribes recorded their depredations, or when they conquered these civilizations and adopted their administrative methods.

Later, thanks to developments in shipbuilding and navigation, Phoenicians and Greeks developed maritime confederations consisting of loose-knit networks of trading settlements, initially in the Mediterranean and later extending into the Black Sea and along the Eastern Atlantic seaboard. 'City-state' joined tribal horde and tribute-empire as a form of polity. More than two thousand years ago an exceptional combination of favourable location, technological ingenuity, and military prowess enabled two of these city-states to transform themselves into empires. Rome benefited from the relative ease of maritime communication in the Mediterranean but this also brought it into conflict with its rival, the Phoenician city-state of Carthage, close to present-day Tunis. By the middle of the second century BCE, after more than a hundred years of war, Rome had gained control of Carthage along with its satellites and their hinterlands. This provided granaries and recruiting grounds in Spain and North Africa: just what was needed for expansion eastward into the Balkan peninsula, Anatolia, Mesopotamia, and Egypt, and northward to the Danube, Rhine, and Tyne. For half a millennium Rome presided over an empire of novel character and unprecedented extent.

When modern Americans and Europeans speak of the ancient world, they generally have in mind this extensive Roman Empire and the Greek-speaking world of roughly the same period. They have been taught that many of their values and institutions can be traced to this crib: the birthplace of Western Civilization with capital W and C, democracy (dubious), language and literary genres (less so). Architectural orders and ideals of public virtue are among the treasures supposedly saved from the wreck. (They might equally well claim tyranny, slavery, and blood sports.) Constantinople, founded in 330 as a new capital for the Empire, lingered within steadily diminishing territories until the city finally fell to the Ottoman Turks in 1453. The decisive fall of Rome itself in 476 has often been taken as the end of the ancient world. In that year Romulus Augustus, last Emperor of the West, was deposed by Odoacer, a Germanic soldier who ruled as King of Italy till 493. The Western Catholic Church survived, claiming universal authority in spiritual matters. A halting attempt to restore the Empire was made by Charlemagne, the greatest of the Germanic princes, who was crowned Holy Roman Emperor by Pope Leo III in 800 CE. The Holy Roman Empire which he established went on to claim temporal supremacy over numerous quasi-independent Central European states with varying success until its abolition by the French Emperor Napoleon Bonaparte in 1806.

In strictly political terms, and within Europe, the fall of Constantinople was taken as the start of the modern world, heralded by consolidation of kingdoms in Aragon, Castile, Denmark, England, France, Portugal, Scotland, and Sweden, to name but a few of the rising states that lay outside the Holy Roman Empire. Together they experienced a renaissance or rebirth of ancient literature, architecture, and culture. The period that separated them from the ancient world could now start to be thought of as the Middle Ages, literally between ancient and modern. Of course, other less grandiose and Eurocentric definitions of modernity abound, usually starting a good deal later than 1453, and many of these stress technological rather than constitutional change as the decisive force in world history.

An example of the sillier kind of contemporary history can be gleaned from the Soviet general who, in the 1980s, explained to his British guests why they were on the wrong side: Moscow was the third Rome. Its historic mission was to defend the values of the ancient world against decadence and barbarity, exemplified in the popular culture, consumerism, and public violence of the USA. Enoch Powell, hyper-realist Conservative member of the British parliament, might have concurred with this view: he believed that the USA was Britain's chief enemy and the Soviet Union its natural ally.

Distaste for American mass culture was indeed widespread among the more romantic sort of British conservative in the mid-twentieth century, guiding the art commissioning policy of Kenneth, later Lord, Clark at the Ministry of Information during the Second World War. This bizarre fantasy of enduring order built around Rome and its successors has been entertained at length, and the term 'romantic' deliberately deployed to demonstrate how history may be misused to invest mundane interest with spurious dignity. The mid-century anti-Americanism of Powell, Clarke, and many in the British Foreign Office, not to mention those Britons who spied for the Russians during the Cold War, arose from patrician repugnance in the face of United States power and resentment at Britain's loss of empire and markets. Those who acted from these petty feelings needed a good story to comfort them and found it in an eccentric interpretation of history. More recently, Venezuelan President Hugo Chavez played a similar game, attempting to reinterpret the history of his country in ways that supported his ambition to integrate South America and balance the power of the USA.

The extraordinary difference made by the presence or absence of tribute-empires was writ large in the history of European empire in Asia and in the Americas, where the Spanish first touched land in 1492. In Middle America (present-day

Mexico and Guatemala) and the High Andes, Cortes and Pizarro encountered elaborate tribute-empires dominated by Aztec and Inca lords and priests. The almost supernatural prestige of the Europeans allowed them to exploit local rivalries and, in effect, decapitate these polities, taking over their administrative and fiscal systems. For British settlers further north (and for Spaniards and Portuguese elsewhere) the absence of existing empires made for a much slower start. It was not until the eighteenth century that serious settlement beyond the coastal belts of North America and Brazil got under way. Up to that time the most lucrative British settlements were Caribbean islands, where near-total elimination of Indigenous peoples following their exposure to European microbes together with the subsequent introduction of African slave labour had allowed large-scale plantations to flourish. In Asia, too, the most spectacular conquests were those of the British. They appropriated the pre-existing Mughal Empire in much the same way that the Spanish had in Mexico and Peru, though after more of a fight. Elsewhere, throughout most of Africa and Asia, the relatively modest scale of political organization offered no easy pickings. The exceptions – China, Japan, Korea, and Thailand – had seen what was coming and made ready, taking effective defensive precautions.

The first odd thing about Western Europe in the modern era was that it remained a patchwork of small states – statelets – resisting the successive attempts of the Habsburgs, the Bourbons, Napoleon Bonaparte, and Adolf Hitler to unite it. Even stranger was the apparent ease with which so many of these relatively small and poor monarchies and republics were able to bridle the empires of the wider world and ride them for so long. Henry Kamen has argued convincingly that the puzzlement of historians in the face of the apparent decline of Spain, notwithstanding the riches of its empire, was misplaced. The point, he insisted, was that Spain had never been rich; there had been no decline.

So how had the Spanish managed to rule an empire stretching from Buenos Aires to California and from Manila to the Gulf of Guinea?

Weakness, not strength, was the mark of the early European states, most of all the English, whose monarchs had little choice but to delegate tasks and powers, which they themselves hardly possessed, to companies formed by gangs of merchants and soldiers. These enterprises were referred to in royal charters as 'bodies politic', and so they were. With delegated rights to govern territory – waging war, issuing currency, maintaining courts and prisons, and imposing taxes – they were serious rivals to the modern nation-states into which they would finally transform or be absorbed. Such were Virginia, Massachusetts, and other colonies on the North Atlantic coast of America, and also the Levant Company trading to the Eastern shores of the Mediterranean or the Eastland Company in the Baltic.

The histories of companies and states intertwine. Soon after its establishment, the British East India Company felt sufficiently secure to refuse membership to the very king who had granted its royal charter. The Eastland Company was established at the request of the King of Denmark in 1579 to bring the English traders and fishermen in his realm to order and oblige them to fund a royal ambassador from Queen Elizabeth of England with whom he could negotiate, something she could scarcely afford. In 1756 Sidi Muhammad, ruler of Morocco, launched a campaign against British shipping, taking many captives. His aim was 'not to … provoke war, but to pressure [the British] into appointing a consul in his country with whom he could do business'.

States might be weak, but in Christian Europe their anointed monarchs had the edge over companies when it came to legitimacy. Moreover, the relative weakness of early modern states was more than compensated for by the ingenuity and technological innovation of their citizens in navigation, military technology, and manufacturing. New sea routes enabled long-distance trade to be conducted, free from the repeated tribute payments that were levied along the old land routes from Asia. Taxation of new commercial wealth and the ability to borrow on newly developed European capital markets allowed European states to develop their military capabilities and pursue their rivalries in a series of wars, increasingly spilling over into Asia and the Americas. This culminated in the Seven Years War of 1756–63, which saw France ousted from North America and India by the British. Close observation of luxury imports from the East enabled the textile manufacturers of Catalonia, Lancashire, and Lyon and the potters of Staffordshire and Meissen to replicate Indian muslins, Chinese silks and ceramics, and even the humble South American poncho. Cheap, but almost always inferior, the resemblance of these European products to the original too often anticipated the gap in taste between a MacDonald's hamburger and an Argentine steak. High-turnover, low-margin uniformity has been the gift of Euro-American industry to the world, enabling millions to live at a level of comfort their ancestors could hardly have imagined.

In summary the history of European empire was less of initial technological and military superiority than of lording it over non-European polities by a combination of quick-witted diplomacy, maritime supremacy, and sheer good fortune: a sprint start that subsequently provided the means to strengthen European states, establish capital markets, build up military capability, and develop manufacturing industry. Only after this reinforcement of their base had been accomplished, toward the end of the nineteenth century, did the European powers start to extend to their overseas dependencies those intrusive forms of government and social surveillance that they had been pioneering at home, prompting local resentment that rapidly developed into nationalist movements, seeking independence.

Empire and Industry

By the end of the nineteenth century the European states-system had consolidated and attained unprecedented levels of administrative capability. As recently as 1850 Central Europe was divided into more than two dozen sovereign states. By 1900 the total number of states in the whole of Europe was no more than this. The consolidation was achieved by the formation of just two new states – Italy and Germany – by 1871. Together they extended over a thousand miles, from Hamburg in the north to Palermo in the south, interrupted only by the small and neutral Swiss confederation, and incorporating most of the territories that had earlier comprised the Holy Roman Empire. Europe was now dominated by just five Great Powers: Austria-Hungary, Britain, France, Germany, Italy, and Russia.

The problem created by this territorial consolidation was twofold. In the first place it made Britain, France, and the Netherlands – parent states of far-flung maritime empires – much more vulnerable at home. This was amply demonstrated in the 1870s by the rapid victory of Germany over France. The first of many German-invasion-scare novels to be published in Britain, *The Battle of Dorking*, was on sale within a year of the formal declaration of the new empire in 1871 and was an instant bestseller. Second, it called into question the viability of maritime empire as an organizational form, suggesting that the future might belong to very extensive continental states with continuous territories.

The United States was close to completing its conquest of a broad swathe of North America averaging roughly 1,000 miles from north to south and more than 2,000 miles coast to coast. The Russians had reached the Pacific as early as 1639, though not until 1891 did they push a railway through to Vladivostock, 4,000 miles east of Moscow. Meanwhile they had taken advantage of dwindling Ottoman strength to encroach into the Caucasus and had strengthened their southern flank by the conquest of a clutch of formerly independent polities. These have re-emerged since the fall of the Soviet Union as Khazakstan, Kyrgistan, Tajikistan, Turkmenistan, and Uzbekistan. Germany, as a late-comer, found few colonial opportunities in Africa and the Pacific. Her future appeared to lie in the creation of a Central European state on the scale of the United States or Russia, ideally in alliance with German speakers in the Austro-Hungarian Empire. France became the first victim of the new German imperialism following the Franco-Prussian War of 1870 with the loss of her north-eastern provinces of Alsace and Lorraine. So the scene was set for more than a century of intermittent warfare and permanent hostility to determine whether domination of the Eurasian landmass could be achieved and, if so, whether by Russia or Germany.

As Europeans and their colonial subjects struggled to make sense of these momentous events, they developed interpretations of history that claimed to explain events and offered justifications for policy. So-called theories (though they were hardly that) of imperialism, socialism, nationalism, and geopolitics flourished from the end of the nineteenth century, occasionally colliding with one another. In Europe there was much soul-searching. How could industrial competitiveness and military capability be maintained? What constitutional and political glue would best hold together the widely dispersed empires of Britain, France, and the Netherlands? How might Spain best respond to loss of empire following the 1898 Spanish–American War?

Much of what Europe achieved was at the expense of non-Europeans, many of whom had become subjects of European states, their industries weakened or eliminated by European exports, their people initially fatally infected or enslaved and later recruited as canon-fodder into the armies of their masters. This ultimately fuelled independence movements that demanded restitution and the reform of the global institutions that they believed perpetuated Northern domination. The recent successes of Brazil, China, India, and Korea, following the trail blazed by Japan, have weakened the frequently heard claims of South American Marxists in the 1960s that development of the world's poorer countries – the periphery of the world economy in the jargon of the day – could be achieved only by violent revolution. Still, it has not quelled resentment. This is just one of many ways in which history, embodied in institutions established by past powers, may continue to have impact even when those powers have faded.

Nationalism was to prove an enduring inspiration in the Global South and the discipline of geopolitics emphasized the influence of material resources and constraints on international rivalries. Although later discredited by the world wars, for which some held it partly responsible, geopolitics preoccupied policy-makers in Europe and the Americas at least to the 1940s, and continued to exert some influence into the Cold War era. It addressed three principal issues: the relative advantages of maritime and continental empire, the likely distribution of power in a world of continental states, and whether security was better achieved by a forward or a defensive posture. A consensus developed around the opinion of English geographer Halford Mackinder (1861–1947) that whoever ruled the Eurasian landmass commanded the world.

The moral drawn by Britain and the USA was that no single state must be allowed to unite East–Central Europe and Asiatic Russia. The relatively greater vulnerability of small economies to depression in the 1930s and the development of long-range bombers and missiles persuaded many, including British former diplomat and pioneer of International Relations E.H. Carr, that the future lay with extensive continental states. The best Britain could hope for was to hold the balance between the USA and the eventual victor of a European conflict. Carr advocated appeasement, first of Germany and later of the USSR. The initial response in the United States, echoed in the trade policies of Britain, France, and Germany during the deep world depression that followed the 1929 Wall Street Crash, had been to envision a future world divided into spheres of influence, each more or less autarkic, or economically self-sufficient. The British had started down this path in 1932 with a policy of imperial preference, favouring trade between the self-governing states within its empire. There was even talk of imperial federation, though the wide geographical dispersal of British territories made its plausibility entirely dependent on naval power and supposedly impregnable garrisons, such as Gibraltar or Singapore. For the French, political union with Algeria and the proximity of their other African dependencies to the metropolis produced a plausible agglomeration on the world map, though Indo-China was a significant outlier. Official minds were preoccupied with large expanses of territory, ideally continuous, as the building blocks of the international system.

Thinking in the US State Department ran pretty much along these lines up to 1941, with Latin America as the obvious sphere of influence from which Britain, still economically dominant in the Southern Cone of America, might progressively be displaced. But the evident vulnerability of the Pacific coast of the USA, demonstrated by the 1941 Japanese attack on Pearl Harbour, its Hawaiian naval base, resolved disagreement in Washington between isolationists, who had favoured hunkering down in the Western hemisphere, and those who favoured a more forward policy.

Nicholas Spykman (1893–1943), Yale IR Professor and Theorist of Geopolitics, agreed with Mackinder's estimate of the importance of the Eurasian landmass. He argued, in his influential 1942 book *America's Strategy in World Politics*, that the fate of the world would be decided in what he called the 'rimlands', which encircled the Eurasian heartland. Ever since, while generally avoiding permanent colonial entanglements, the USA has concentrated its military bases and personnel in a great arc from

Japan to Germany. Its major military commitments, both direct and financial, have been consistent with Spykman's expectation: hot wars in Korea, Vietnam, and Iraq; proxy wars in the Middle East and Afghanistan; military support to Israel and Egypt; and bases in Germany, Italy, Japan, Korea, and Turkey. During the 1960s almost all of the 7.6 million United States troops serving abroad were stationed in Europe or East Asia. Over the second half of the twentieth century fifty-two percent were in Europe and forty-one percent in Asia. US troops were concentrated within Spykman's 'encircling buffer zone'. Such is the power of theory.

Dealing with recent history in terms of geopolitics involves focusing more on grand strategy, less on commerce and investment, and leaving aside values and ideology altogether. The victors of the world wars claimed to have fought for democracy against autocratic or totalitarian states. At least in the first phase of the Cold War, the USA set out to rally all peoples of faith against Godless Communism. Much was rightly made of the evils of the Soviet system of labour camps – the Gulag – and of the hideous industrialized extermination by Nazi Germany of Jews, Gypsies, and homosexuals. Not only did these states deserve to lose, their ideologies were thought to have hampered their effectiveness. Soviet murder of so many of their own high command in 1937 and German anti-Semitism resulted in serious losses to fighting effectiveness and the war economy. Conversely, the final victory of the Western Allies was attributed in part to their values.

Democracies might be slow to anger, but once roused they were superior war machines because their peoples shared the values of their leaders and their capitalist economies were flexible and responsive to wartime exigencies. The case was put with particular eloquence a few years after the war by Swedish economist Mancur Olson, who argued that Britain had twice survived efficient naval sieges because social solidarity allowed a very effective system of rationing to work. In addition a general mobilization of women had compensated for numerical inferiority and kept the war economy running, something impossible in Germany because it clashed with traditional German 'home and hearth' ideology. Moreover, by delaying rearmament until it was absolutely necessary, the liberal democracies had avoided the costs of premature redirection of their economies and stockpiling while gaining military advantage through incorporation of the latest technological advances into their weapons systems.

As a result of their emphasis on national interest and power, political realists are inclined to disregard ideology. The geopolitical dilemmas facing Germany, Russia, and the USA in the twentieth century would still have had to be resolved even if the belief systems of each had been reversed or were identical to one another. Policy, realists insist, was dictated by enduring national interests arising from the position of each country and the balance of power in the states-system. Outcomes were determined by the distribution of power or, to use the more comprehensive term, of capabilities. What this bleak view neglects is that ideas are embedded in institutions that prove, in the event, to be more or less effective when pitted against one another. Totalitarian states, whether nationalist or communist, turned out to promote institutions that were less effective than those of the capitalist liberal democracies. So it was that the Soviet Union finally collapsed in 1991, unable any longer to bear the strain of trying to match the USA.

This event brought to a close more than forty years of uneasy peace. The alliance systems led by the two superpowers, NATO and the Warsaw Pact, had stood in readiness for conventional warfare in Central Europe. Millions held their breath when periodic crises provoked increased levels of military readiness: the Berlin airlift of 1948, the 1956 Soviet invasion of Hungary, the 1962 Cuban missile crisis, the Prague Spring of 1968, and the final German crisis in 1989.

Beyond Europe it seemed that virtually every state or liberation movement enjoyed the patronage of one side or the other, though Yugoslavia and China were able to stand to one side of the game after breaking with the USSR in 1948 and 1960 respectively. In divided Korea, Russia and China backed the North, and the USA and its allies, the South. In Vietnam it was much the same, though US President Richard Nixon (1913–94) began a rapprochement with China in 1972. In South Asia the USA opted for Pakistan and the USSR for India. In the Middle East the USA plumped for Israel while the USSR provided more cautious and selective support for the Arab states. As the Portuguese Empire in Africa fell apart after the revolution of 1974, Cuba and the USSR supported the communist successor governments in Angola and Mozambique while South Africa and the USA backed anti-communist insurgent groups. Even in strategically marginal South America, Brazil worked closely with the USA, leading to talk of sub-imperialism, while disgruntled Argentina, punished by the USA for neutrality in the Second World War and mistrusted as a direct competitor in temperate-zone farm products, sold its grain to the Russians. In some cases this superpower patronage resulted in proxy wars; in others, merely in stalemates and inconclusive posturing.

The end of the Cold War, in 1989, created political space in which some of these confrontations could be resolved, but the chief consequence of Soviet defeat was that the USA became the strongest military power in the world. The US economy has remained among the largest, though gradually giving way to newly industrializing countries (NICs). This has led to much debate. Some think this balancing is a universal characteristic of any international system. Others regard it as less common in the long run than informal arrangements in which lesser powers cluster around a leader, such as China was for many centuries in East Asia. This is another subject on which IR theorizing reflected and commented on current affairs, as policy-makers after 1989 pondered how long the USA could remain the world's sole superpower. More recently the rapid economic growth of Brazil, China, and India, while posing no immediate military threat to the USA, has prompted debate about the sustainability of these emerging industrial societies. Their implications for carbon emissions and global warming, their effects on land use and ecological balance, their ability to satisfy rising expectations and respect individual rights are all matters of grave concern, as is the ability of even the most highly developed states to maintain complex transport, communications, and power systems indefinitely and defend them against cyberattack and natural disaster. The 2011 post-earthquake leakages of radioactivity from the Fukushima reactors in Japan, a well-established industrialized economy, showed the danger.

Reconfiguration of the state was a second consequence of the end of the Cold War. The worldwide selling off of state assets to private-sector corporations is not so very far removed from French and Belgian seizure of German rolling stock, locomotives, and heavy machinery in 1918, or the customary looting practised in earlier wars. As in the past, weak states have been further weakened by sales in which state assets were frequently undervalued, allowing the victors and their new friends to profit richly.

Meanwhile, beyond the zones of social order and economic growth, the costs of modernity are evident in the plight of those people whose states and entrepreneurs have failed to meet its challenges. In some places the state itself has become a predator. Perhaps worse, in so-called failed states there is no monopoly over the legitimate use of organized violence. In many parts of sub-Saharan Africa clean water, drains, and regular electricity supply are not to be had, and regular employment is so scarce that a child's best chance of survival to adulthood may be to turn soldier or risk premature loss of life working in an illegal mine. Heading the list of failed states in 2012 were the Democratic Republic of Congo, Somalia, and Sudan. Outside Africa but high on the list stood Haiti, Afghanistan, and Yemen. Between the zones of order and disorder swirl trafficked labour, demoralizing drugs, small arms, cyber fraud, charitable handouts, journalists, blood diamonds, resentment, and sympathy.

Histories: Universal, Conjectural, Modern, and Contemporary

There are many different kinds of history, each told with a different purpose and each claiming to offer a different sort of lesson. Priests and philosophers used to offer strongly interpretative histories that suggested a direction in which human affairs are going, for good or ill. Foremost among these in the Christian world has been the concept of divine providence, under which all of human history is seen as the expression of an omniscient creator-God, from the fall of man in the Garden of Eden, through the redemptive life of Christ, to the day of judgement. It is a version of this grand narrative that motivates Christian Zionist support for the State of Israel today: another example of policy-makers seeking theoretical support. Other lesser schemes have included Marxist characterization of history as a dialectical class struggle, in which successive phases – bourgeoisie against aristocracy, workers against bourgeoisie – legitimized the use of organized violence.

The paramount lesson of universal history seems to be that you might just as well go with the flow, but this is so subversive of effective action and social discipline that both the Catholic Church and the Communist Party sought ingenious ways to motivate the faithful, notably through the doctrine of justification by works and the theory of the vanguard party. Realists in IR have drawn a second lesson from universal history. This is that all eras, being part of a single story, are comparable to one another. It follows that Thucydides is still relevant to policy-makers today. To anyone thinking this way it made perfect sense for General Schwarzkopf to base his campaign against Iraq on Carthaginian tactics against Rome at the Battle of Cannae in 216 BCE, though no one seems to have pondered the strategic disaster that subsequently befell victorious Hannibal, stranded in Italy with overextended lines of communication. For many realists change within historical time is superficial and the lessons of history are timeless.

Universal history blends with conjectural history when the teller moves from interpretation of what is known to speculation about how things must have been and, by implication, what must be still to come. Early modern European political theorists spilt much ink arguing about the origins and nature of the state. Was it some kind of implicit contract by which individuals in a stateless world relinquished their freedoms in the hope of attaining security, or was it a forcible and ultimately unnecessary imposition on perfectly viable savage societies by a band of brigands who invested themselves with the dignity of kingship? The first option sits well with a liberal view of international relations; the second, with the realist view. Whether the state is seen as the final guarantee of security or the ultimate threat to it is likely to make a difference to one's political opinions, though less than might be thought to one's political behaviour. In history, as in political theory, it is not hard to identify sources of contemporary realist and liberal approaches to international relations.

The thumbnail sketch of the first five millennia of world history offered in the first section of this chapter is an example of universal history, dealing with the whole of human history as a tale of civilizations rather than of individual polities, and less concerned with events than with material drivers and structural constraints. However it tries to resist intrusive interpretation. The section on more recent times that followed had more the character of *modern* history, though its implicit choice of 1871 as a start date is open to challenge. Few people now date modernity from the fall of Constantinople in 1453, but many still prefer a relatively remote date. In 1648 the Treaties of Westphalia, held by many to have inaugurated the modern states-system, were signed, and this date is a favourite with writers on international relations. Many general historians opt for the 1789 French Revolution, which destabilized Europe by causing irreparable harm to monarchy and Church. Economic historians often prefer some date close to 1830, after which industrialization began to be widely experienced throughout Europe and beyond, in the form of steam-powered transport and machinery. Others would think 1871 too early. There is a case – shortly to be advanced – for 1961, the year in which the test explosion of the Soviet fifty-megaton Tsar Bomba inaugurated a nuclear stalemate.

What defines modern history is not so much that it begins in any particular year, as that it moves steadily forward from that point to describe a project – modernity – and its achievement. Sometimes stress is placed on the nation-state, a pattern set by John Motley's classic 1855 *Rise of the Dutch Republic*. Sometimes the stress is on technological and economic advances. Always the hallmark is progress. Modern history is progressive history. This is both its attraction and its vice. It promises too much. It leads its readers up a path strewn with good intentions. For those whose main concern is international relations, the dating of modernity has an additional significance. How like our own times does the past have to be in order to offer useful lessons? Realists incline towards universality. Fundamental structures do not change. Liberals, believing in progress, are more inclined to dismiss appeals to pasts that they find too different to be helpful.

The contrast drawn by Geoffrey Barraclough in 1961 between modern and contemporary history complements this distinction between realist and liberal uses of history, the latter reaching back to the sources of current problems and the former providing narratives to vindicate the present. Its name suggests that contemporary history must be exclusively concerned with events of the very recent past. Quite the contrary: it works backwards from contemporary problems to disclose their origins, in the hope that these may suggest solutions. However, it scours the past for information specifically relevant to the problem under investigation, not for timeless systemic features.

A contemporary history of racial tensions in a North American or European city may need to reach out halfway across the globe to understand values and institutions developed in countries from which immigrants reached the USA in the course of more than three centuries. To try to understand differences between the USA and Britain over gun laws and attitudes to firearms is to enter a political minefield. How and when did the right to bear arms evolve into widespread ownership and recurrent abuse of firearms? Was it in the revolutionary period or after the Civil War? To understand the hesitancy of wealthy London Jews to take responsibility for poverty-stricken co-religionists arriving in the city in flight from ethnic cleansing (pogroms) in Russia at the end of the nineteenth century one needs to understand the struggles of the Spanish-speaking (Ladino) Sephardim to gain legal emancipation and social acceptance in England and the profound cultural distance that separated them from their Yiddish-speaking Ashkenazi cousins.

The essence of contemporary history lies in the embeddedness of past events in present-day institutions and law. Its value is more likely to lie in understanding a problem than resolving it, but understanding is a start. As a method, it may lead inquiry back beyond the start of modern history, and to parts of the world remote from the problem to hand.

If the characteristic vice of modern history is its progressive bias, that of contemporary history is primordialism. The primordialist seeks to challenge current rights and institutions with claims drawn from the past, but neglects the need for the past to be entrenched in current practices in order to have continuing significance. Does pale skin and being brought up in a former slave port make someone the debtor of present-day African-Americans or members of the long-established black community of Liverpool? Not a bit of it. The ancestors of the man or woman in question may have come to the city long after trade was banned and the slaves emancipated. Even if they did not, they might just as easily have been anti-slavers, or for that matter slaves, as slavers. Besides, many of the Liverpool black community were never slaves or, if enslaved, only briefly. Some traded their own countrymen and women; others were mariners, serving in the British navy. Some became partners in Liverpool merchant houses. The search for authenticity is a wild goose chase.

This conclusion is easier to accept for some than for others. Those who live in status quo states will have little trouble with it. Among the dispossessed, the passage of time may not make it any easier to abandon claims for redress, apology, or compensation. In the opening of Robert Fisk's 1990 book on Lebanon, he discusses the keys with which Palestinian refugees had locked their front doors when forced into exile in 1948. When Fisk met the refugees in 1977, these keys were considered powerful symbols. But so long as the locks were not changed and the houses still stood they were more than symbolic. It might one day be possible to go back, which is just what a group of Lebanese civilians did in 2000, defying Israeli troops by marching into an occupied zone and reclaiming homes seized twenty-two years before. But such possibilities of restitution seldom extend beyond a lifetime, if that.

Yet time does not heal all wounds, and ancient resentments can be fanned into life, like the embers of a fire. This happened in the Balkans in the 1990s, setting Orthodox Serbs, Catholic

Croats, and Bosnian Moslems at one another's throats. A similar rekindling has bedevilled the Middle East for more than a century, since the Zionist movement first gave practical political expression to Jewish claims to the biblical territory of a pre-Roman Jewish state.

The only credible legal basis for the State of Israel is the 1917 Balfour Declaration. In this letter to Lord Rothschild, a leader of the Jewish community in Britain, British Foreign Secretary Arthur James Balfour made no mention of a Jewish state, but did express support for the establishment of a Jewish homeland in British-controlled Palestine. This commitment was subsequently elaborated in the 1920 Sèvres Treaty, between the victorious powers of the First World War and the Ottoman Empire, and by the League of Nations Mandate that formalized British occupation of Palestine in 1923. Neither the Old Testament nor the continued presence of a Jewish minority under Roman, Arab, or Ottoman rule adds any legal force to Jewish statehood. Israel was the outcome of modern decisions by modern statesmen. It cannot be underwritten by history, and to claim that it can needlessly complicates a tough international problem that is hard enough to digest without nostalgic garnish.

More akin to the claims of Palestinian exiles than those of modern Jewry are the appeals for retrospective justice of the bereaved, the tortured, and the imprisoned in Argentina, Chile, South Africa, and Spain, where long periods of dictatorship or tyranny were accompanied by massive human rights abuses. But it is noticeable that, in each case, many have preferred to expose the truth and provide compensation rather than to seek punishment of those responsible, for fear of upsetting fragile democratic settlements. The Spanish case has been an especially prudent exercise in selective memory. Silence was maintained for an entire generation following the death of the dictator Francisco Franco in 1975. Only in the last ten years have mass graves been opened up as the grandchildren of the republican dead have felt it safe to interrogate the past.

It is important to distinguish between claims for restitution or compensation and claims about causation. Placing the causes of a current conflict in the remote past takes the weight of today's horrors from the shoulders of those immediately responsible for them. During the Balkan wars of the 1980s there were those who claimed that this was all that could be expected of people who had ancient enmities wired into them and were timed to explode at the first opportunity. But Mladić, Milošević, Karadžić, and Krstić were not hapless victims of an age-old struggle, but fully responsible agents. The causes of these wars are plain to see in the constitution introduced by President Tito in 1974 and in the loss of legitimacy his death visited upon this recent and artificially constructed state. In this case being South Slavs – a merely linguistic commonality – turned out to be an insufficient cultural basis for sustained political community. To allow each state in the federation to clear foreign payments independently and maintain its own militia was to invite trouble, given continuing cultural and religious differences. Memories of Chetnik and Partisan war crimes in the 1940s, historical fantasies woven around Bosnian Cyrillic script, and the symbolic value of the Kosovo battlefield, where the Ottomans had defeated the Serbs in 1389, were grist to the mill, but no more. They helped community leaders to raise emotional intensity but did nothing to justify contemporary claims.

Cultivated Forgetfulness

The best defence against misuse of history is to be aware of it without leaning on it. In a fine essay, the German thinker Friedrich Nietzsche suggested that effective action often required forgetfulness: not a failure of memory but a deliberate casting aside of memory. One of the best practical ways to achieve this is to draw a distinction between the recent or contemporary past and the more remote past. The treaties of Osnabrück and

Münster, which brought an end in 1648 to thirty years of devastating warfare in Europe, have often been regarded as the point at which a recognizably modern system of states came into being in Europe and hence the start of modern international relations. This Westphalian system was supposedly made up of a number of sovereigns, each ruling over a defined territory or realm, within which lived a discrete population. The population owed loyalty to the sovereign, who exerted exclusive jurisdiction and temporal authority over them and was able to marshal national resources and deploy them strategically. Will this do as a starting date for contemporary history? No, because it is parochial and Eurocentric, and because the international system has since come to be dominated by much larger entities, both states and corporations, than those it legitimized.

How about 1870, which is quite close to the dates chosen by Barraclough, coiner of the term 'contemporary history', half a century ago, and by future Soviet leader Vladimir Ilych Lenin, writing in 1917? There are two arguments in favour. The first is that the consolidation of European states, the global rivalries between them, and the rise of the USA and Russia as continental powers marked a sea change in the international system. The second justification is technological: the internal combustion engine, electricity, powered flight, high explosives, penicillin, typewriting, cinema, and submarines were all in the offing. But again the answer must be no. Jets, rockets, electric motors, pilotless drones, genetic modification, television, and the internet have followed in the wake of Barraclough's foundational innovations. The only debt of the computer to the typewriter is its keyboard.

If 1648 and 1870 fail to provide adequate starting points for the contemporary world, other candidates remain. In 1961 the Soviet Union tested a nuclear device far exceeding in explosive power all the weapons used in the Second World War. Coinciding with the peak of decolonization, this event made clear the final shift from a Eurocentric world of territorial empires to a global system in which the framework of security was defined by weapons of mass destruction and long-range delivery systems. It also confirmed a bipolar structure that was to endure till 1989. This immediately poses the question of whether mutual deterrence or bipolarity was the decisive cause of peace during the Cold War. If it was bipolarity, then the world entered a new phase with the collapse of the Soviet Union in 1991 and the move to unipolarity. If it was nuclear deterrence, then the structure established in 1961 endures, though now multipolar, and on the brink of further proliferation. One argument in support of the claim that mutual deterrence has been the defining feature of the contemporary era is the pervasiveness of what are often called 'new wars'. Fear of the devastating consequences of war between nuclear powers, triggered by intervention in local conflicts, did not prevent UN participation in the Korean War (1950–53), US support for South Vietnam against the communist North (1964–73), or Soviet suppression of reformist movements in Hungary (1956) and Czechoslovakia (1968). However, nuclear weapons may be said to have influenced the outcomes of these conflicts by restricting the freedom with which the superpowers could deploy conventional forces, contributing, for example, to the survival of communist Cuba just eighty miles from the USA.

Together with decolonization, awareness of this constraint on the use of force by major powers has been among the causes of a vast upsurge of public violence across large parts of the world, most notably in the recently relinquished dependencies of the European states. There, AK47s and Kalashnikovs have long abounded alongside the ubiquitous machete. More recently, in the heartland of the 'old' Atlantic world, the 11 September attacks on east-coast United States targets in 2001, the bombings at Madrid's Atocha railway station on 11 March 2004, and those in London on 7 July 2005 have extended the zone of insecurity. Periodic interventions by leading powers have failed to quell this endemic problem. Russia has waged intermittent warfare in the

Chechen Republic since 1994 and suffered terrorist attacks in its heartland from Chechen rebels. The Moscow theatre hostage crisis of 2002 cost the lives of more than forty Chechen fighters and 136 hostages. The Soviet Union spent ten years trying to subdue Afghanistan, from 1979 to 1989; the USA and its allies have been there for more than a decade, since 2001. The 2013 murder of an off-duty British soldier, Lee Rigby, in a London street was justified by those accused of his murder as retaliation for the victims of British arms in Afghanistan and Iraq.

On the technological front 1961 is a good enough date, if a shade early, to capture the advent of transistors, satellite communications, the beginnings of computing and the internet, the cracking of the genetic code, the internationalization of production and banking, the development of global brands, and cheap air transport, bringing mass tourism and unprecedented labour mobility. If we turn to economics, 1961 catches the beginnings of discontent with the postwar global economic order and the acceleration in levels of international transactions we call globalization. It is as good a date as any to mark the high tide of decolonization. On the other hand, to suggest 1961 is to ask more than half the world's population to accept, as contemporary, a period starting well before they were born.

Forgetting history turns out to be less about ignorance of the past than the cultivation of an acute awareness of precisely what it is about past events and dilemmas that make them relevant or irrelevant to the present. Using history intelligently requires an ability to sense which of the circuits seeming to link past and present are still live, which dead. In the early years of the new millennium the Chinese government got this wrong. They hoped to replace rapidly waning Marxist ideology with an enhanced sense of national identity as a source of stability during a period of rapid change. They publicly recognized the long-suppressed role of the nationalist Kuomintang forces in the 1937–45 war against Japan, but this led to a wave of public resentment because it also exposed the sustained maltreatment of Kuo Min Tang veterans following the 1949 victory of the Communist Party over its nationalist rivals.

History offers vindicatory narratives and analogies: situations bearing a structural resemblance to current predicaments. But it only takes a small difference for a vindication to bite back or for an argument by analogy to be rendered irrelevant or, worse, misleading. History offers lessons, but policy-makers need to kick their tyres carefully before driving off. Philosophers distinguish between necessity and contingency. Necessary truths are those that are true by virtue of the meaning of their terms, for example 'All bachelors are unmarried'. Most claims about the world are contingent: they may or may not turn out to be true. Europeans thought that all swans were white until they found black swans in Australia. History offers no necessary truths. So the greatest benefit of extensive study of history is not an ability to find ready-made solutions to contemporary problems but to develop an appreciation of the uncertainties in current assumptions and practices, and encourage innovative political thought and action. Policy-makers need to be constantly on the watch for black swans.

3
The global economy

Military defeat of the United States in Vietnam in 1973 coincided with the most serious economic crisis since the Second World War. Towards the end of the long postwar boom, strong demand for primary commodities such as oil and copper had led to a surge in prices. This allowed oil-exporting countries, through OPEC, to quadruple oil prices in 1973–74. This decision was driven in part by the determination of oil-rich Arab states to sap Western support for Israel. These events led scholars on both sides of the Atlantic to pay closer attention to international economic relations, and to the interaction between states and markets. In the past, political realists had tended to be preoccupied with the affairs of state, leaving private social interaction, including trade and migration, to liberals. The gap between the two positions is sometimes unhelpfully summed up in terms of politics and economics; but this crude distinction neglects the fact that states cannot function without resources, while production and exchange are impossible without some level of security. Suddenly, economics was felt to be too important to be left to the economists, and International Political Economy emerged as a new academic field, to complement or transform more traditional forms of International Relations. The question was no longer whether to concentrate on states or markets – politics or economics – but which of the two was paramount.

Do states ultimately dominate the world by their ability to use legitimate authority to set the terms on which commerce can take place? Is the prevailing balance of power projected on to or derived from the global economy? Supporting the former suggestion is the provision of reserve currencies by the most powerful states, such as the US dollar, until recently the sole currency used for global trade in oil. There is further evidence in the predominance of established powers in the voting systems of International Financial Institutions (IFIs) and the terms imposed by those institutions on weak states as a condition for financial assistance. Or is it the other way around, with states only able to function by the consent of the governed, manifested in the willingness of peoples and corporations to fund them through taxes and bonds? Are liberals right to think that accelerated rates of economic growth can be achieved through unrestricted international trade, investment, and migration? Even if they are, can growth on these terms be sustainable and equitable? Can it be achieved without irreversible environmental degradation, a fatal loosening of the bonds that hold society together, and the subordination of states to vast global corporations? Are wars fought to enhance national wealth, or are they instead a drag on the economy? What kind of country is most effective in war? Is it one with tight state control over national resources, or one in which citizens and firms have relative freedom from state interference? Does globalization herald the demise of the state, or merely its reconfiguration? Up to 1968 the US dollar was as good as gold; by 2013 its gold value was little more than two percent of the 1968 figure. Firms in the USA controlled fifty-seven percent of global foreign direct investment in 1970; by 2010 this figure had fallen to twenty-eight percent. In 1973 the value of total US international trade in goods stood at roughly 10% of total output of the economy (Gross Domestic Product or GDP); by 2006 this had more than doubled, to 21.8%. The world had clearly changed; but were these figures symptomatic of national decline or welcome evidence of a more liberal and vigorous economy?

Typical answers to all these questions have varied a good deal over time. The account provided here starts by establishing the institutional framework within which current international economic interactions take place. It next outlines the main features of recent globalization. Only then does it look back in time, tracing the origins of ideological positions that still underlie rival policies today.

Bretton Woods and the Southern Response

International economic relations still bear the marks of the 1940s postwar settlement. From the earliest stages of the Second World War, officials in the warring states debated the structure of the postwar world economy. In Allied circles it was widely believed that economic dislocation and depression in the interwar period had fuelled extremist political parties. Their territorial and commercial ambitions, in turn, had poisoned international relations during the 1930s, culminating in war. Economic stability was therefore regarded as a matter of common concern not simply for its contribution to welfare but as a guarantee of security. The Soviet Union had detached itself from the capitalist system, so it fell to the United States and Britain to provide leadership at the Bretton Woods conference of July 1944, where the outline of a new monetary and financial system was agreed. At its heart were two novel institutions: the International Monetary Fund (IMF) and the World Bank (formally known as the International Bank for Reconstruction and Development). Regulation of the global monetary system, once a matter for privately owned banks, was now a matter of state.

The primary function of the IMF was to ensure the stability of exchange rates and the convertibility of the world's major currencies, thereby avoiding the damage that had been suffered by world trade following the 1933 devaluation of the US dollar. When country A devalues, its exports immediately appear cheaper to buyers in country B, who are able to buy more country-A currency than before with each unit of their own. Conversely, exporters in country B find that their own goods are now more expensive in country A and may seek relief from their own government. The rational response of a national government in country B is to try to avoid an adverse trade balance by a devaluation that matches or exceeds the first one. But individual rationality produces collective insanity as political action substitutes for market exchange, and in the 1930s this led to a vicious spiral of competitive devaluations and protectionism. You might almost say that economics is about reducing your own costs while politics is about increasing those of your rivals.

The postwar monetary system was designed to avoid any repetition of this disaster. Given the size and strength of the US economy, the system was constructed around the dollar, which had been fixed at $35 per ounce of gold in 1934. The commitment to maintain this rate meant that world trade in commodities such as oil could be conducted in US dollars, free of the risk of currency instability. The central purpose of the IMF was to help maintain exchange rate stability by providing resources to protect national currencies when they came under pressure. Each member state was assigned a quota, which determined its entitlement to borrow and its voting power in the Fund's executive board. The USA, with forty percent of the votes, had an effective veto. By the 1960s this had reduced to a little over twenty percent, but it still constituted a built-in veto since important decisions required a four-fifths majority.

The World Bank, meanwhile, had been designed to fund postwar reconstruction, but as relations with the Soviet Union soured and Europe began to divide into hostile camps, the USA decided to undertake this task unilaterally through the 1947 Marshall Plan, which devoted more than $13 billion to Europe, while more modest transfers were made to Japan.

It had been intended that the third pillar of the postwar economic order would be the International Trade Organization, but the US administration was unable to secure domestic support for this, and the world fell back on the 1947 General Agreement on Tariffs and Trade (GATT). The interwar economy had been torn apart by trade protectionism, exacerbated by competitive devaluations. Tariffs (or taxes) on imports had long been a valuable source of income for poor countries with weak states and had been used in the USA and Germany in the nineteenth century to help infant industries. In the depression of the 1930s the governments of Britain, Canada, Germany, and the USA, among others, bowed to pressure from manufacturers in mature sectors of the manufacturing industry, notably textiles, who were coming under severe pressure from imports produced in newly industrializing countries such as Japan. With the imposition of restrictive import quotas and a resort to interstate barter trade, the global trading system degenerated to the point where the world economy was seriously disrupted. United States policy-makers were determined that this should not happen again. Intended as no more than an interim arrangement, the GATT held the fort until the creation of the World Trade Organization (WTO) in 1995. The GATT banned quotas and fostered the principles of non-discrimination and reciprocity. No barrier should be imposed on one country or group of countries and not on others; a concession made to one should be extended to all. The GATT also provided a forum for successive rounds of negotiations in which average tariff levels were reduced and residual non-tariff barriers began to be addressed.

Together these organizations established monetary and trading regimes that stood the capitalist world in good stead for a generation, presiding over a period of unprecedented prosperity in Western industrialized countries and faltering only towards the end of the 1960s, as it became impossible for the USA to sustain the convertibility of the dollar. The system was based on the conviction that capitalism required careful management by states, both domestically and internationally. It was flexible, allowing periodic devaluations against the dollar by major currencies, the retention of quotas restricting trade in some sectors, and the exclusion of agricultural goods and regional free trade arrangements from the strictures of the GATT. The exceptions made clear that security came before welfare. Permitting the formation of the European Economic Community in 1958 is the best example of this. As a customs union this imposed a common external tariff on goods from outside its borders; conversely international trade between the members of the union was unrestricted (in theory). This clearly disadvantaged exporters from outside the union and breached the GATT principle of non-discrimination. It could lead to global loss of welfare through trade diversion, as consumers within the customs union bought locally produced goods in preference to more efficiently produced goods from outside the union, made more costly only by the tariff. But the positive aspect of this, at least from the perspective of labour, was that US-based TNCs were drawn into local manufacture behind the common external tariff by the prospect of access to a very large market. Besides, some economic sacrifice was justified on geopolitical grounds. The strategic purpose of the European Common Market, predecessor of the European Union, was to meet the Soviet threat by providing a structure within which German industrial recovery would not be thought threatening by France.

By the 1960s decolonization had changed the composition of the UN General Assembly, which became one of the key locations from which a reaction against the Bretton Woods system was launched. Newly independent countries together with the established Latin American republics formed the Non-Aligned Movement, at Bandung in 1955. Increasingly, as the euphoria of political independence gave way to the realities of poverty and underdevelopment, the new Asian and African states turned their attention to inequities in global economic regulation.

In its early years the IMF had been drawn on by a relatively small number of countries. By the mid-1960s membership stood at over a hundred states, but more than half the drawings on the fund had gone to just five countries: Brazil, Britain, France, India, and the USA. Four-fifths of the relatively small percentage drawn by Third World states had gone to just a tenth of their number, mostly India and Nationalist China (Taiwan). The chief reason for this was that the IMF would not lend unless a borrowing state agreed to conditions which appeared, to less developed countries (LDCs), to take inadequate account of the many ways in which their economies differed from those of the developed countries (DCs). In advanced industrial countries states had a wide range of fiscal and monetary tools at their disposal. The typical Third World country had a weak tax system and little option but to make heavy-handed use of monetary policy if it was to comply with IMF conditions, needlessly depressing the economy.

Robbed of its original task by the Marshall Plan, the World Bank had taken up the challenge of assisting the economic development of LDCs. Few of these countries could afford to borrow at prevailing market rates in hard currencies. They might all too easily see the value of their own currency deteriorate against the US dollar or Pound Sterling during the life of the loan or fall victim to a rise in interest rates, making repayment more burdensome. Moreover, the Bank, like the Fund, imposed conditions on its loans, including the adoption of policies favourable to private enterprise and economic openness. The situation improved a little following the establishment of the

International Development Association in 1960, an affiliate of the World Bank that loaned to Third World states on easier terms. But most developing countries had to rely for their development on bilateral transfers at subsidized rates from Britain, France, the USA, and other developed countries. These transfers were often tied to the purchase of armaments or construction equipment from the donor, or used to provide an outlet for costly agricultural surpluses. Sometimes aid seemed to be flowing from poor to rich, and what's more, to the former colonialist states.

Together the states of the Global South used their strong position in the UNGA to establish a new body, the United Nations Conference on Trade and Development (UNCTAD). By contrast with the Bretton Woods institutions, UNCTAD was dominated from its inception by a coalition of Third World states, the Group of 77 (G77), so called for the number of founder members. Though membership of UNCTAD was open to all UN member states, its secretariat was, on the whole, ideologically aligned with the G77, and its function was to put forward proposals for reform that were generally blocked by twenty-nine developed countries that made up Group B. Many of the proposals were ill-conceived. The idea of a common fund to stabilize the prices of internationally traded primary commodities (such as sugar, coffee, and cocoa) was premised on a group insurance principle: when some prices went up, others would remain low. But primary commodity prices tend to move in parallel, in response to cyclical demand. This said, UNCTAD and the more general North–South dialogue of the 1960s and 1970s provided a diplomatic training ground for future leaders of the Global South, notably India and Brazil, while also creating an atmosphere of reform in which some small gains were made. In 1966 the developed countries adopted Part IV of the GATT and agreed to avoid increases in barriers to goods from less developed countries. They also established an International Trade Centre in Geneva to provide information and training for officials from the South. Meanwhile the IMF increased the quotas of its less developed members and introduced a Compensatory Finance Facility in 1963 and Special Drawing Rights in 1969. The first of these provided some insurance against instability of export earnings, calculated to benefit exporters of primary commodities. The second promised to inject greater liquidity into the monetary system, though this was a promise that did not amount to much; it was soon dwarfed by the availability of cheap dollars from commercial sources for medium-income states.

The close of the 1970s saw the North–South dialogue stalled for a combination of economic and geopolitical reasons. The collapse of the fixed-rate monetary system came towards the end of a long postwar boom in the Western economies, at which point a short-lived rise in the prices of primary commodities gave false hope to the Global South. It also placed large sums of money in the hands of oil-exporting states. Oil was traded in dollars, but the oil-rich states were at loggerheads with the USA over Israel and preferred to place their dollars in accounts beyond US jurisdiction, as did communist China. But banks cannot just sit on deposits. If they are to pay interest to depositors and make a profit for their shareholders they simply have to lend; and lend they did! Middle-income countries in Latin America and elsewhere found it possible, from the mid-1970s, to borrow at advantageous rates from commercial banks. Reform of the IFIs began to seem less urgent.

The end of the long postwar boom was followed by a period of uncertainty in the West, during which there was much talk of US decline, a possible return to the kind of multipolar international system that had existed before 1914, and a recurrence of protectionism. There were straws in the wind. Firms that benefited from protective tariffs in their home markets could afford to sell in export markets at or below the cost of production in order to maintain production at levels that would avoid a rise in unit costs and idle productive assets. Colloquially referred to as dumping and very common in the interwar years, this was prohibited under the GATT. Suspecting dumping, the USA started to impose Voluntary Export Restraints on Japanese and European steel makers from 1968. The GATT prohibited quotas, but there was nothing to stop importing states from asking exporters to limit exports voluntarily. The 'volunteering' was clearly being done under the threat of anti-dumping actions in the courts that would, if successful, exclude imported steel altogether. To exporters it made sense to keep reduced access to the US or European market rather than none at all.

If the world economy was in a delicate condition, so too was world politics. Revolution in Iran had ousted that country's hereditary leader, or Shah, Mohammad Reza Pahlavi (1919–80), a long-time ally of the United States. In November 1979, after the Shah was granted asylum in the USA, Iranians occupied the US embassy in Tehran in protest, holding its staff hostage for more than a year. The following month the Soviet Union invaded Afghanistan. The new year saw mounting protests in Poland against the Soviet-backed communist government. In October the following year, under pressure from the Soviet Union, the Polish Communist Party installed former defence minister Jaruzelski as prime minister. He, in turn, sought a Soviet guarantee of military support should his resort to martial law fail to restore order. The Soviets declined, all too aware of the sanctions that would be imposed by the West if they invaded Poland.

An April 1980 US mission to free the Iran hostages failed ignominiously. At one and the same time a breach in US containment of the Soviet Union was threatened in Central Asia, while Soviet resolve seemed to be faltering in Central Europe. Meanwhile, the Global South was pressing for institutional reform and the world economy was awash with cheap money. It was in the midst of all this, at the start of the 1981, that Ronald Reagan took office as president of the USA, determined to reverse perceptions of US decline by standing firm against the Soviet Union.

The great complication, from the point of view of international economic relations, was that the steps taken by Reagan to strengthen the domestic economy and US military capabilities had profound implications for the global economy. Throughout the industrialized West the late 1970s had seen very high levels of inflation. In the United States average price rises exceeded eleven percent in 1979 and thirteen percent in 1980. Early in the new presidency Paul Volcker, chairman of the Federal Reserve, raised interest rates in order to quell inflation and fill the gaping hole in the budget left by major tax cuts. The US prime interest rate, which provided the benchmark for other rates, was raised to 21.5% in June 1982.

This increase in interest rates had a catastrophic effect on countries in Latin America and beyond that had borrowed dollars heavily from commercial banks. These loans were generally for periods of three months, renewable; but the terms were set afresh at each renewal in line with prevailing interest rates. Rising US rates made the burden of debt service unsustainable. In October 1982 Mexico defaulted on its loans, and was soon followed by others. The debt crisis that ensued forced many of the leading states of the Global South into the hands of the IFIs. Between them the Fund and the Bank were able to enforce drastic reforms as conditions of bailouts, and the debtor state had no option but to comply with the conditions imposed under this so-called Washington consensus, because the commercial banks were unwilling to join in any renegotiations that lacked official blessing. State-owned enterprises, notably public utilities providing telephone systems and electricity generation, were privatized. Mostly they were sold off to transnational corporations. The revolt of the South was effectively at an end.

After a decade of ignominy and indecision – the defeat in Vietnam, the exposure of Richard Nixon – the United States rediscovered its historic mission, which was to defeat the Soviet Union. Even to have flirted with the North–South dialogue had been a distraction and a symptom of national weakness, now cast aside. By 1986 Mexico, once a voluble Third World leader, had joined the GATT; by 1993 it had signed the North American Free Trade Agreement (NAFTA) with Canada and the USA, enabling goods to flow freely from the Guatemalan border to the Arctic Ocean.

For reasons that will soon become apparent, international economic relations since the 1980s have often been termed 'neo-liberal'. Though they are connected, the meanings of 'liberal' in political and economic discussions are not identical. Political liberalism centres on the emancipation of the rational individual from the bonds of tradition and arbitrary authority. Economic liberalism is characterized by minimal state interference in the operation of markets. This is clearly consistent with political liberalism, since one of the things most rational individuals choose to do, once emancipated, is to make money. The additional twist in economic liberalism is the claim that rational individuals, each competing with the others, will inadvertently achieve the best available collective outcome, and certainly a better outcome than will come from any form of planning.

It is certainly true that many states throughout the world have privatized, deregulated, and opened their economies over the past twenty-five years. Currencies have been allowed to float, their value determined by commercial dealers. The removal of obstacles to trade has continued. And all this has been done by political parties of every ideological variety, including the Chinese Communist Party, Margaret Thatcher's Conservatives and Tony Blair's New Labour in Britain, and traditionally populist Peronists under President Carlos Menem in Argentina. To this extent recent decades have seen a flowering of neo-liberalism. But the liberalization has been selective and incomplete. To begin with, the whole process has been imposed by powerful institutions and states, and the reforms have too often been formulaic and inappropriate. Secondly, it has been a sham in many of the richer states, which have been left with scarcely reduced revenues at their disposal. Often their spending has merely been redistributed from direct subsidization of the private sector to support of the economy through the provision of infrastructure, healthcare, and an educated workforce. In many instances this transformation has been accompanied by forms of social surveillance and discipline inconsistent with the fundamental emphasis of political liberalism on individual freedom. Thirdly, it has taken place in a world in which the scale of corporate organization is quite unprecedented. This has meant that TNCs have gained more from the process than individuals.

The Dimensions of Contemporary Globalization

The circulatory system of the world economy consists in movements of goods, people, and capital across state frontiers. Since the 1990s levels of international transactions relative to those within national frontiers have surpassed pre-1914 levels. One of the most impressive statistics in support of this view is the ratio of merchandise trade (exports plus imports of goods) to GDP for the United States. Because of its sheer size and the complementarity of its regional economies, the United States used to register low figures for this ratio compared to developed European economies.

The low ratio for 1950, shown in Figure 2, reflects a general dislocation of the world economy caused by protectionism in the 1930s and war in the 1940s. But it is the figure for 2006 that is startling; it registers the effects of increased trade by the USA within the North American free trade area, and with NICs such as China and India. It also conceals a mounting US trade deficit, sustainable only so long as the dollar remains an important reserve currency for other countries and a leading medium of exchange.

1913	1950	1973	1995	2006
11.2	7.0	10.5	19.0	21.8

Figure 2 Ratio of United States merchandise trade to GDP at current prices, 1913–2006
Source: Paul Hirst and Grahame Thompson, *Globalization in Question* (Cambridge: Polity, 1996), p. 27, Table 2.5, citing A. Maddison, 'Growth and Slowdown in Advanced Capitalist Economies', *Journal of Economic Literature*, 25:2, 1987, Table A-23, p. 695, for 1913, 1950, 1973, and 1995, and the US Census Bureau for 2006.

This growth in trade is linked to a profound change in corporate organization over the same period. Cross-frontier trade between the component elements of large corporations – so-called intra-firm trade – was thought to account for a third of Japanese and US exports by the end of the 1990s and fully two-thirds of US imports from Mexico, where so-called *maquiladora* (screwdriver) plants carried out the labour-intensive stages of manufacture of goods destined for the US market. Neo-liberal reforms from the 1980s made it easier for large private corporations to operate internationally. This coincided with the development of new information technologies, which made global production systems cheaper and more robust, and with substantial reductions in barriers to trade. A third element in the drive to corporate globalization was the development of new markets, as the numbers of middle-class consumers in China, India, and other NICs burgeoned.

Foreign direct investment (FDI) is the export of capital over which the investor retains managerial control. It typically takes the form of the acquisition or establishment of factories, mines, or other productive assets that complement a firm's existing business, and therefore serves as a rough measure of the growth of the world's TNCs. The pattern of international FDI up to the 1980s was for the largest manufacturing corporations in the leading industrialized economies to invest abroad. They did this to secure raw materials and cheap labour or to leap tariff walls, exploiting markets approximating those of their home countries. Usually such firms continued to concentrate research and development in a home market that accounted for a substantial proportion of total sales. This was especially true of United States firms, given the extraordinary size of their domestic market. The recent development of more integrated global strategies can be seen in Figures 3, 4, and 5. The figures show that TNCs based in countries such as Germany, the UK, or the USA have been confining their operations to the developed core of the world economy. They also show a significant rise in the proportion of inward FDI coming from outside the established industrialized economies. The rise in non-traditional sources of FDI, notably China, is a significant element in a combined flow that has quadrupled over the past twenty years.

Alongside merchandise trade and FDI, related financial transactions between major financial centres have also grown, and this has been identified as one of the key qualitative changes that distinguish recent globalization from pre-1914 economic integration. Figure 5 shows rises in transactions in bonds and equities. Bonds represent loans to corporations, states, and other public authorities on which interest is paid; equities represent the capital of corporations, entitling their holders to a share in profits and capital growth. When compared to the national economies in which they take place, these transactions have increased much more than cross-frontier trade in physical goods or investment in productive assets. So too has trade in financial derivatives, typically depending on future values of assets.

Together these deals bear testimony to two important aspects of contemporary globalization. The first of these is the increasing role of services, including financial services, relative to the production of raw materials and their transformation into manufactured products; the second is the unprecedented concentration of these services in global cities, in many ways more closely integrated with one another than with their local hinterlands.

Foreign Direct Investment and Global Trade in Securities

	1990	2000	2010
Outward	93	88	82
Inward	75	76	65

Figure 3 Share of developed countries in world stocks of FDI (%age), 1990–2010
Source: UNCTAD STAT (http://unctadstat.org).

	1970		1980		1990		2000		2010	
	($bn)	(%)	($bn)	(%)	($bn)	(%)	($bn)	(%)	($bn)	(%)
World	14	100	52	100	241	100.0	1232	100	1171	100
Developed economies	14	100	48	92	230	95.0	1095	89	851	73
USA	8	57	19	37	31	13.0	143	12	329	28
UK	2	14	13	25	18	7.0	233	19	105	9
China, incl. Hong Kong	0	0	0	0	2	0.5	60	5	144	12

Figure 4 Outward flows of FDI in US $ billions at current prices and exchange rates, and as %age of world total, selected years 1970–2010
Source: UNCTAD STAT (http://unctadstat.org).

	1980	1990	1998
USA	9	89	230
Japan	8	119	91
Germany	7	57	334

Figure 5 Cross-border transactions in bonds and equities as %age of GDP, 1980–1998
Source: J. Perraton, 'The Global Economy – Myths and Realities', *Cambridge Journal of Economics*, 23:2, 2001, p. 674, cited by Warwick E. Murray, *Geographies of Globalization* (London: Routledge, 2006) p. 67.

Transnational Corporations and Global Markets

The advent of truly global corporations is one of the most prominent features of recent globalization. Yet for all the talk of pulling back the state and allowing free rein to market forces, corporations on this scale should give pause to those who characterize the most recent phase of globalization as neo-liberal. To do so is at the very least ironic. One of the targets of early liberalism in Britain, at the turn of the nineteenth century, was the power of large corporations – most of all the mighty East India Company. This giant could impose barriers to market entry and dominate the legislature to the detriment of smaller enterprises and the consumer. It was a battle the pioneering liberals won, only to see a new form of corporation emerge.

The nineteenth century saw progressive advances in metal-working, allowing machinery manufacturers to turn out interchangeable parts, any complete set of which could be assembled to produce a standard item. Cheap printing and distribution of newspapers and catalogues using national postal services and railway networks made it possible to advertise a range of products regionally or nationally, while rising incomes further enlarged the market. The result was a general move from local workshops making unique products to clients' specifications towards larger factories producing standardized items with recognized brands. Before long, multi-plant firms emerged. The next step was for one or more of a firm's plants to be located outside its country of origin.

Trade had been international for centuries, but dispersed industrial production under a single corporate management was something new. One early example is the firm of Samuel Colt, established in Hartford, Connecticut, to manufacture the Colt revolver in 1848. A display demonstrating the interchangeability of its parts at the 1851 London Great Exhibition confirmed the

Colt's reputation, and European demand was sufficient to justify setting up a branch plant in London in 1855. A second case, with particular implications for women, was the sewing machine. The Singer Manufacturing Company began mass production in the USA in the 1850s and soon established a strong reputation and brand loyalty. It followed Colt across the Atlantic in 1867, when it set up a branch plant in Glasgow, Scotland. By 1884, when it moved to a new factory in nearby Clydebank, its seven thousand workers were turning out more than thirteen thousand sewing machines each week.

The initial effect of this new device was the ability to economize on (largely female) domestic labour, formerly responsible for making and mending the clothing of family or neighbours. The increased availability of the sewing machine rapidly led to the relocation of the manufacture of clothing into small factories. These were often justifiably called sweatshops, anticipating clothing factories throughout Asia today. They made standard items in standard sizes for distribution through the new department stores that were replacing traditional drapers throughout Europe and North America. Some seamstresses (even the word, like 'draper' or 'wheelwright', is almost defunct) stuck to their trade, buying a sewing machine and working at home for a small circle of middle-class clients. More joined the army of low-paid factory machinists. Better-off women used the availability of ready-made clothing – together with canned foods, and domestic appliances such as refrigerators and washing machines – to economize on their time and that of their servants. They were able to substitute leisure or employment in other, better-paid, sectors of the economy for domestic drudgery. Before long, most of the servants would also be dispensed with.

All this had incalculable social consequences and is why the sewing machine is emblematic of late nineteenth-century social change. To take just one example, until the 1870s clerks throughout the world of commerce and finance were almost

Figure 6 The wartime mobilization of women
Source: 'We Can Do It!' poster for Westinghouse Electric, closely associated with Rosie the Riveter, Wikimedia Images.

uniformly male and relatively highly paid. By 1900 their work had become much more routine as vast halls equipped with typewriters and adding machines replaced the more intimate counting-houses immortalized in the novels of Charles Dickens. A major element in this transformation was the appropriation of shorthand note-taking and typing by women. Clerking had become clean and respectable work for the lower middle class. In this way the whole range of domestic appliances helped make possible the typing pool. Women's growing participation in the public sphere helped prepare society for the much larger role they would shortly play in war economies.

The history of the automobile has features in common with that of the sewing machine. Coach-builders and agricultural engineers were already standardizing their products towards the end of the nineteenth century. Horse-drawn public transport was beginning to extend the practical range of urban commuting, supplementing the railways and canals. But it was the introduction of internal-combustion engines to road vehicles, starting in Germany in 1888, that was truly revolutionary. Mass production followed within a decade. Within half a century automobiles and coaches had eliminated the much more labour-intensive infrastructure that had been needed to support draft animals across half the world. The land required for fodder, the grooms and stable-boys, and the stud farms and pastures were redeployed. Most of the horses were less fortunate. In their place, the automobile required a massive response from states and the private sector alike. Locally, wheelwrights and blacksmiths retooled as motor mechanics. Globally, public investment in national road networks needed to be matched by the development of reliable supply chains from newly discovered oilfields in the Dutch East Indies, Iran, Russia, and the United States to every settlement of any significance throughout the world.

Harvard economist Raymond Vernon, writing in the 1960s, produced a schematic history of products such as the sewing machine and the automobile. It helps explain their initial implications for international trade and corporate structure and the qualitative changes in trade and investment of the past half-century. It is based on a standard abstraction that has been fundamental to classical economics since the time of David

Ricardo (1772–1823). In his *Principles of Political Economy* Ricardo observed that all production required the combination of three essential factors: land, labour, and capital. In the Europe of Ricardo's day, each of these was supplied by and closely identified with a distinct social class: aristocracy (landowners), proletariat (workers wholly reliant on their wages), and bourgeoisie (townspeople with property).Vernon's product cycle started from the idea that innovations reflected the relative costs of the factors of production.

In the late nineteenth century incomes in the USA were relatively high and skilled labour was relatively costly, so innovations that economized on it did well. Such innovations were also affordable to enough consumers (the remaining skilled workers) for their production in bulk to be profitable and their cost kept affordably low. Mass production typically requires considerable investment in the design of a new product, setting up a production line, advertising, and organizing its distribution. If a firm is to survive and prosper it must recoup these costs. The initial pricing of each unit of production will therefore include an element assigned to defray so-called sunk costs, and reflect an assumption that sufficient units can be sold at the designated price to cover them. The more units that can be sold, the lower this element of the price can be set. Set the price too high and competitors will under-cut it. Set it too low and sunk costs will not be covered. This is one reason why global trade in aircraft, where an order for twenty or thirty more units can make the difference between profit and loss on the whole product run, has traditionally been so corrupt. Bribes of a few million here or there pale into insignificance when compared with the financial consequences of selling a couple of dozen planes too few.

It is no accident that global firms first emerged in countries with large domestic markets. The economics of mass production favoured long product runs, which made possible the powerful combination of heavy investment in product development coupled with an affordable retail price. This explains why the US market quite rapidly saw the elimination of smaller producers of motor vehicles and the emergence of an oligopoly – a small number of sellers – comprising Chrysler, Ford, and General Motors. Once the US market had matured, so that the bulk of new demand was from people replacing their vehicles, rather than first-time buyers, the battle between these three centred on market share, which determined unit costs, which in turn determined profitability. It was this market structure in the USA that was to determine corporate behaviour in the next phase of the product cycle.

The economic structures of other countries, especially in Western Europe, began to resemble those of the USA as incomes rose relative to other factors of production. Rising demand for vehicles was met at first by local manufacturers, such as Renault in France or Fiat in Italy. US firms could take a share in these markets by exporting, but transporting vehicles was expensive and in the nationalistic climate of interwar Europe states were inclined to impose import taxes, especially on the products of industries they were keen to develop because of the employment they offered and their strategic importance. Fiat is a case in point, as a state-owned company in a slightly laggardly industrialized country keen to mechanize its armed forces. But a second reason was that relative factor prices in Europe, though convergent with those in the USA as labour costs rose, still favoured smaller, lighter vehicles because land remained more costly. For an economist 'land' includes the land occupied by roads and factories, but also the materials used in the manufacture of motor vehicles and the petroleum that fuels them. In all respects land was cheaper in the USA than in congested Europe. If they were to do business there, US firms therefore had either to develop distinctive products for the European market or else acquire existing European manufacturers. So why didn't the Big Three in the USA simply leave the European market to the Europeans? The reason was that European markets were growing more rapidly than the US market, offering opportunities to earn accelerated income that could be used to increase market share in the much larger US market. If one of the Big Three started to manufacture in Europe the others were bound to follow, which is exactly what happened.

In spite of the early lead of US firms, European competitors were able to get a foothold in their own markets, often with government assistance. The motor industry could be regarded as strategic, both because of the role of motor vehicles in conventional warfare and because of the large numbers of workers employed. What was true of Europe applied even more to Japan. There, labour was relatively cheap while 'land', especially energy, was expensive. So the Japanese developed very compact, light vehicles that were perfectly positioned to break into the US market in the 1970s when energy prices there rose sharply. Yet the addition of Fiat, Honda, Toyota, or Volkswagen to the US trio of Chrysler, Ford, and General Motors did not substantially alter the structure of the world industry, which consisted in an oligopoly in which every firm depended substantially on its country of origin. The more recent global presence of manufacturers based in India, Malaysia, and elsewhere does not fundamentally change the picture. What lies behind the globalization of the last thirty years is a structural transformation in this and other sectors of the manufacturing industry. The automobile industry remains oligopolistic, but the oligopoly is less concentrated and more complex than before. Production – both in general and within each firm – is much more widely spread; inter-corporate alliances are common; and the range of products is much more finely calculated to exploit niche markets and encourage multiple vehicle ownership by wealthy households.

Globalization has been accompanied by a dispersal of power as new corporations have emerged in rising economies such as Brazil, China, and India. But this can easily be over-emphasized. *Fortune* magazine's 2011 list of the world's 500 largest corporations includes only 133 based in the USA and as many as 61 with headquarters in China. But closer examination shows that many of the top 500 are primarily active in their home market, while many of the leading US firms are more genuinely global in the range of their activities. A list of leading companies in declining order of overseas assets, provided by the *Economist* (10 July 2012) on the basis of UN figures, makes the point very effectively. Heading the list was US-based General Electric, with seventy percent of its assets and more than half its workforce outside the USA. The next three firms on the list were oil companies – Royal Dutch Shell, BP, and Exxon Mobil – based in the UK/Netherlands, UK, and USA respectively. The major Latin American and Asian state oil companies do not figure on the list, where the top twenty are almost exclusively US and European firms (with just two from Japan).

Structural change has also been evident in sectors other than manufacturing, reflecting the lighter touch of the neo-liberal state. Privatization of public utilities and the opening up of sectors such as petrochemicals and communications media offered great opportunities for global diversification in the 1990s. Banking, for example, has seen the emergence of larger corporations with global presence. This is evident at the retail level. Global brands such as Barclays, HSBC, or Santander are able to offer commercial banking facilities to personal and corporate clients worldwide; HSBC converts the supposed cultural sensitivity implied by its global presence into an intangible asset, featured in their airport advertisements. More significant, however, has been the integration of commercial banking, mortgage lending, investment banking, portfolio management, and exchange dealing in single institutions. This was widely blamed for the banking crises of 2008–11 in the USA and Britain.

Trade in primary commodities is another sector that has changed radically in recent decades. These commodities range from oil and coffee to heroin and cocaine. For much of the twentieth century states made great efforts to control the prices of durable internationally tradable commodities. The prices for such goods were generally volatile, responsive to the cyclical boom-and-bust pattern of the world economy. Sugar is a good example. The bulk of world sugar in the early twentieth century was sold on long-term contracts between exporter and importer states. This made for extreme price variation in the residual free market. Major producers first addressed the problem collectively in response to the depression that followed the US stock market crash of 1929. Sugar had fallen from its pre-crash peak of 7 US cents per lb to just 1.5¢ per lb. The 1931 Chadbourne agreement, named for US corporate lawyer Thomas Chadbourne, who led negotiations between Cuba, Java, and the major central European sugar beet producers, established export quotas and production cuts. This was followed by further international agreements in 1954 and 1958. In spite of these agreements, the world price rose from 2¢ per lb in 1962 to almost 12¢ per lb the next year, only to fall back to 4¢ per lb in 1964. The following year – in response to the extreme price volatility of the preceding three years – sugar became one of the first commodities regulated under the United Nations Conference on Trade and Development, which had been established only the year before.

By the 1970s the USA objected to restrictive commodity agreements on principle because they interfered with the free play of market forces. But the falling away from attempts to regulate global markets that followed was not simply ideological. It reflected repeated failure. International commodity agreements had depended on pacts between exporter states to limit exports or release stocks in such a way as to keep the free-market price within agreed limits. One problem was that stability, generally at slightly too high a price, encouraged new entrants. A second difficulty was that US ideological objections had been reinforced by the political behaviour of oil-exporting states in the 1970s. War between Israel and its Arab neighbours in 1973 led the

Organization of Arab Petroleum Exporting Countries (OAPEC) to cut off oil supplies to states supportive of Israel. At the same time OPEC exploited a tight world market by quadrupling the price of crude oil from $3.00 to $11.65.

This combination of explicitly political use of commodity power and commercially motivated market manipulation hardened US opposition to attempts to manage world commodity markets. In subsequent decades the International Sugar Organization and similar organizations have been reduced to a largely statistical and monitoring role, while TNCs have become more active in commodity trades. Price instability persists in residual markets, aggravated by the increased share of large corporations in the total trade. Coffee, to take one important example, experienced two spikes in the 1990s, with nominal prices for Arabica coffee briefly rising from a typical range of between $1 and $2 per kilo to $5 or $6. John Baffes and his co-authors refer to this as the operation of distortion-free markets in a 2005 World Bank publication. This is misleading. Liberalization of markets has been asymmetric, with relatively few effective curbs imposed on the growth or disruptive effects of corporate power.

The global clothing industry has seen similar deregulation. Trade in textiles was excluded from post-1945 attempts to liberalize world trade because of the industry's vulnerability in developed industrial economies to rising competition from newly industrializing economies. Successive agreements, reluctantly signed by mature producers such as Brazil, India, and South Korea, promised annual increases in the quotas admitted to developed-country markets. Quotas were extremely specific by country and product. A game ensued in the 1970s and 1980s in which DCs shifted quotas from established exporters to new entrants in expectation that they would not be able to exploit them fully, while nimble entrepreneurs shipped machinery from one country to another to ensure that, for example, that year's Mauritian shirt quota for the EU was not wasted. By 1994 agreement had been reached to phase out DC quotas, but the DCs continued their rear-guard defence of an almost vanished industry by reserving some of the most important concessions to the end of the ten-year transitional period. Subsequent years have seen a free market in which China has been a formidable competitor. In this less tightly regulated world, clothing and footwear designers and retailers with strong brands in DC markets have been able to locate manufacturing in highly competitive low-wage countries, mostly in East Asia, risking reputational damage through possible association with under-age and coerced labour.

Illegal drugs and people trafficking come last in this survey of corporate growth. Here DC regulation has remained, motivated by concern for well-being. Cocaine, heroin, and the traffic in people have had deplorable effects in the USA and Europe, and though local criminals bear substantial responsibility, international gangs have been increasingly active. There has been extensive debate about the division of responsibility for these trades between exporter and importer countries. A case in point is the trade in women from Vietnam and Burma into China to serve as brides. Here the root cause lies in Chinese policy a generation ago, when restrictions on family size provided incentives for sex-selective abortion, leading to the current surplus of males. It has even been suggested that abnormally high savings rates, as Chinese parents prepared to fund the purchase of brides, may have aggravated global trade imbalances since the 1990s. Any attempt at state control, as any good liberal will tell you, is like squeezing a balloon. What you try to grip simply turns up elsewhere; distortion begets distortion.

In order to evade the law, criminal gangs increasingly need to control the whole chain of supply. This has led to the development of strong vertically integrated organizations such as the drug cartels in Colombia and, more recently, Mexico. Violently competitive, each such organization benefits hugely from attempts by public authorities to eliminate its trade, always providing that the axe falls on one of its rivals. This in turn constitutes a powerful motivation to suborn law enforcement officials. Though probably accounting for no more than one percent of world trade, trade in drugs and trafficking of people foster accumulations of capital that are typically reinvested in legal construction and property, enhancing the power of organizations that remain corrupt and corrupting at heart.

Liberal Narratives

A standard anglophone narrative of world history concentrates on the spread of modernity from a point of origin in north-west Europe, starting at the end of the eighteenth century. Technological innovation was converted into sustained growth by the division of labour and progressive extension of markets. State interference delayed the process to begin with but was gradually swept aside, first in Britain and then more generally. This facilitated rapid growth of an integrated world economy in the third quarter of the nineteenth century. The process slowed down as deteriorating relations between the political elites of Europe found popular support, fuelled by corrupt and sensationalist daily newspapers. Imperialism and economic nationalism led to war, and the requirements of total warfare during the first half of the twentieth century reversed the economic trend. Growth and international integration then recovered in the postwar decades before accelerating markedly from the 1980s, stimulated by neo-liberal policies.

This narrative is unambiguously liberal and draws heavily on classical political economy. Thinkers of the eighteenth-century Enlightenment began to speculate that a change in the balance of power between monarchs and aristocracy and the rising commercial and industrial classes would constrain the ability of the former to continue their system of warfare. It didn't work out that way, and the subsequent history of liberal thought about the world economy has alternated between confident prediction of bright futures and anguished apologies for their failure to arrive.

In 1784 the German philosopher Immanuel Kant wrote an essay under the title 'Idea for a Universal History with a Cosmopolitan Purpose'. He closed by noting that there were 'reasons of state' for allowing increasing freedom to citizens to engage in economic activity. Social and economic circumstances had arisen in which military success abroad depended on a growing tax base. But the economic growth needed to provide this required liberalization at home, which would gradually place sufficient power in the hands of bourgeois (middle-class) subjects for them to be able to constrain the militarism of the absolute monarchs of Europe. Thomas Paine put forward a remarkably similar argument less than ten years later, in 1791. That Kant – a reclusive German philosopher – and Paine – an English professional revolutionary – should have agreed so closely suggests that these ideas were already common currency. But it was the English textile manufacturer and parliamentarian Richard Cobden who applied this novel theory of class conflict to greatest practical effect a generation later, in the 1840s, when arguing against the protectionist tariff levied on the importation of grain to Britain, under the so-called Corn Laws.

Cobden's attack on protectionism rested on the ideas of his fellow parliamentarian and economist, David Ricardo, who maintained that global welfare could be maximized provided each country concentrated on producing the goods it could make most efficiently. The novel and counterintuitive part of his theory of comparative advantage, and the reason for its name, was the claim that even if one country produced everything more efficiently than another country their *combined* welfare would still be increased by trade, since this would permit each to shift resources into those activities in which it had comparative advantage. What mattered was the relative efficiency with which each good could be produced within each national economy, not the absolute cost advantage of production in each country for any single item. Suppose, for example, that country A can produce a family car using resources costing $12,000, whereas country B can produce an identical car at a cost of $16,000. Suppose also that it costs country A $14,000 to produce thirty metric tons of rice, while country B can produce the same quantity for $15,000. It is clear that country A has *absolute* advantage in both sectors, motor manufacture and agriculture. If each country produces one car and thirty tons of rice, their total production costs sum to $57,000. But if country A specializes in cars, producing two vehicles at a total cost of $24,000, while country B opts for rice production and turns out sixty tons for $30,000, then the total costs incurred in the two countries fall from $57,000 to $54,000, leaving a margin for a profitable exchange. Throw in economies of scale and international trade begins to look very attractive. Yet the advantages of trade have seldom been obvious to those called on to bear the costs of adjustment, be they Detroit car workers or Mexican smallholders. The consequence has been that states have not only been tempted to place obstacles in the way of international trade, but have also tended to act as regulators of the level of monopoly in each national economy rather than opposing it outright.

Efficiency was not the only consideration. There were two distinct aspects to free trade. The first was that neither taxes nor non-tariff barriers, such as health restrictions or government purchasing policies, should inhibit international exchange. The second was that states should neither create nor permit monopolies that excluded competition from a market. Barriers to market entry were every bit as pernicious as barriers to trade. Only free and fair markets would ensure best use of global resources. Such was the liberal gospel.

Accordingly Cobden saw economic liberalization not simply as an exercise in economic rationality, but also as a two-pronged weapon against the aristocracy and their privileged grip on wealth and power. The theory of comparative advantage was inseparable from a liberal theory of class struggle. As landowners, the aristocracy relied for their private incomes on rents paid by their tenant farmers. By removing tariff protection from British cereal producers, Cobden and his colleagues hoped to undermine the big landowners by reducing the ability of their tenants to pay high rents. They also planned to attack the aristocracy's position as exclusive governors of the state and as militarists. Wars had to be funded, and abolition of the Corn Laws removed one important source of revenue from the government of the day, namely the proceeds from the tariff on imported corn. Furthermore, any substitution of direct taxation on incomes for this indirect tax would make taxation more visible to the taxpayer and thereby encourage wider public scrutiny of policy and participation in the political process. Free trade, then, was conceived of as furthering trade by promoting the international division of labour and creating a beneficial interdependence between nations, and also by undermining a belligerent and exclusionary ruling class.

Cobden's campaign against the Corn Laws, which succeeded in 1846, is only the best-known moment in a lifelong campaign for free trade which included significant progress in the general reduction of tariffs across Europe in the 1870s. In the mid-nineteenth century liberals had cause for optimism. Cobden had brought together two powerful lines of argument for free trade, the first that it would permit the unrestricted operation of comparative advantage, and the second that it would end government by self-perpetuating elites. Since the 1980s self-styled neo-liberals have been careless in their recollection of basic liberal principles, recalling the first of these lines of argument and forgetting the second. The frustration of liberal hopes in 1914 and the selective memory of neo-liberals have a common source. It is the unanticipated growth in the scale and power of business organizations or, less convincingly, of labour organizations relative to states, in some ways taking the place of the old aristocracies.

The rising European middle classes had tried to abolish war while making a good profit. Towards the end of the nineteenth century it was becoming clear that they were doing rather better at the second than at the first, but after 1870 the mood changed. The sudden and total defeat of France by Prussia that year, followed by the creation of the German Empire and the final unification of Italy, touched a nerve. The following year George Chesney's *The Battle of Dorking*, a Conservative fantasy set in the near future, envisaged Britain suffering a similar fate to France at the hands of Germany. It proved to be a bestseller: the paperback edition sold around one hundred thousand copies in its first year. Chesney's novella initiated a spate of fantasies about imagined military disasters. The *War of the Worlds*, H.G. Wells's 1898 novel about a Martian invasion, was the logical conclusion. One major theme of the genre was that the Liberal Party had weakened Britain by their policy of free trade. Reliance on imported foodstuffs following the repeal of the Corn Laws had accelerated a flight to the cities. It had not only hurt the aristocracy and made Britain vulnerable to blockade, but had also denuded the country of the peasantry that had traditionally provided its infantry and the yeomen who had filled the middle ranks.

As the century drew on, even Cobden had had to admit that history was no longer going quite as expected, and much liberal thought of the later nineteenth and early twentieth centuries was devoted to accounting for this and prescribing remedies. Faced with deteriorating economic conditions, arms racing and alliance building in Europe, and a scramble for colonies in Africa and Asia, liberals were inclined to save their theory of history by supplementing it with a theory of the inadequacy or corruption of the bourgeoisie.

In Britain the debate was brought to a head by the Boer War of 1899–1902. This may almost be thought of as Britain's Vietnam: a struggle that soon developed into irregular warfare as the fronts dissolved and the Dutch Boers (literally farmers) formed small, highly mobile mounted units, the so-called commandos, to strike at British communications. The decision to deal with Boer guerrilla tactics by denuding the countryside of non-combatants, who were herded into concentration camps, brought widespread censure across Europe and at home when malnutrition and disease struck Boer women and children. The possibility of German intervention on behalf of their Dutch-speaking cousins loomed. How had it come to this?

Of all English liberals, it was J.A. Hobson who provided the most widely read and influential answer in his 1902 *Imperialism: A Study*, a book that would be read with interest and approval by Russian revolutionary and future leader V.I. Lenin. Like other writers of the time, Hobson used the term 'imperialism' to discuss tendencies towards war between the European powers, of which competition for colonies was only one. Hobson traced this recent general deterioration in inter-state relations to two related sources: under-consumption and the influence of business on government. Hobson rejected the assumption from classical economics that every seller would always find a buyer at some mutually satisfactory price, with the result that markets would always clear. Instead he argued that in conditions of extreme income inequality, as in the England of his day, the rich would over-save and the poor would be unable to consume all that was produced by the national economy. A surplus of savings would accumulate in the hands of the bankers; a surplus of manufactured goods, in the hands of industrialists. Both would seek outlets overseas, below cost if necessary. In this way, under-consumption would lead to dumping.

When several national economies tried to do this at the same time, the result was bound to be severe competition for third-country markets and high levels of tariff protection for domestic markets. This was because manufacturers, especially those least competitive in developed-country markets, resorted to political lobbying when defeated in the market, egging on their governments to annexe African and Asian territories within which they might enjoy exclusive market access. Simultaneously –

and to much greater effect – financiers would press governments to provide security, by annexation if need be, in those overseas countries where they had invested the excess savings of the rich. Sharing the commonplace anti-Semitic views of the time, Hobson exaggerated the extent of Jewish control over investment banking, which he regarded as a literally degenerate form of capitalist enterprise. Together, industrial and finance capital were able to suborn the popular press and whip up popular support for their schemes.

Liberal Anti-Semitism

Never let it be thought that liberalism has been a wholly pacific and benign ideology, or racism entirely confined to the political Right. The pervasiveness of anti-Semitism within European liberalism was palpable.

Among his arguments against hereditary authority, Tom Paine noted the tendency of aristocracy to degenerate. He added: 'By the universal economy of nature it is known, and by the influence of the Jews it is proved, that the human species has a tendency to degenerate, in any small number of persons, when separated from the general stock of society, and intermarrying constantly with each.'

A century later J.A. Hobson saw Jewish financial firms as the decisive influence on European politics: 'An ambitious statesman, a frontier soldier, an overzealous missionary, a pushing trader' – he claimed – 'may suggest or even initiate a step of imperial expansion, may assist in educating patriotic public opinion to the urgent need of some fresh advance, but the final determination rests with the financial power.' Hobson continued, in a memorable, often-quoted, and wholly inaccurate passage: 'Does anyone seriously suppose that a great war could be undertaken by any European state, or a great loan subscribed, if the house of Rothschild and its connexions set their face against it?'

Hobson's view of the bourgeoisie found an echo in Vienna, capital of the Austro-Hungarian Empire, where political economist Joseph Schumpeter (1883–1950), writing during the

First World War, faced the same problem. How could capitalism, which had appeared to be a force for peace, have failed to prevent the outbreak of the war, or perhaps even contributed to it? Schumpeter's answer was that imperialism, which he defined as an 'objectless disposition on the part of a state to unlimited forcible expansion', arose because of the incompleteness as well as the corruption of capitalist development. Opposing the Marxist view that class struggle between bourgeoisie and proletariat was now the central historical drama, Schumpeter pointed to the continuing relevance of *past* class relations, embedded in contemporary social values and institutions: what he called 'social atavism'.

The atavism, or reversion to type, with which he was most concerned was the survival into the modern era of powerful remnants of the aristocracy, whose very reason for being lay in waging war. The monarch or nobleman, he claimed, 'wages war in the same way as he rides to hounds – to satisfy his need for action'. This survival was only possible because the capitalist class had been corrupted and had consequently failed in their historic mission to oust the aristocracies of Europe. Elements of the bourgeoisie had been nurtured from infancy by the still imperial state.

Dependence on government purchasing power determined the politics of a great swathe of industrialists, from arms manufacturers through textile manufacturers to construction firms. Others gained by lobbying for and receiving tariff protection, which enabled them to glean a surplus in the domestic market. However, the relatively small size of their domestic markets made it rational for such firms to optimize unit costs by extending product runs, even if the surplus had to be sold overseas at cost, which could be accomplished provided they had access to protected colonial markets. Schumpeter believed that fierce competition in third-country markets was generating pressure on states to annexe such territories and erect tariff walls around them. In 'The Imperialism of Social Classes' [1919] he maintained that 'we have here, within a social group [large entrepreneurs and high financiers] that carries great political weight, a strong, undeniable, economic interest in such things as protective tariffs, cartels, monopoly prices, forced exports [dumping], an aggressive economic policy, an aggressive foreign policy generally, and war, including wars of expansion with typically imperialist character'. Conflicts 'born of an export-dependent monopoly capitalism', he added, 'may serve to submerge the real community of interests among nations'.

For all their criticisms of capitalism, Schumpeter and Hobson remained discernibly liberal. They were convinced that political liberalism and capitalism could be saved by judicious reform. For Schumpeter, this required a more complete capitalist revolution and the political neutering of the aristocracy. For Hobson it required an abandonment of *laissez faire* or domestic non-intervention, one of the sacred principles of classical economic liberalism. Under-consumption and over-saving, the twin engines of imperialism, could be corrected by judicious state management of the national economy in the form of redistributive taxation and the provision of basic welfare. The path was open to liberal advocacy of macroeconomic management and the welfare state.

Hobson and Schumpeter had emphasized close relations with the state as a key element in the corruption of the bourgeoisie. Less prominent in their work, but well to the fore in that of the Russian Marxist V.I. Lenin, was the sheer scale of enterprise. Lenin was less interested than his liberal contemporaries in collusion between states and firms. Though grounded in Marxism, his wartime essay on imperialism juxtaposed elements of contemporary geopolitics and United States populism. For more than thirty years, populists in the USA had been pleading the cause of small capitalists and farmers against the trusts or oligopolies that had come to dominate the US economy. As a Marxist, Lenin thought less in terms of economics and politics than of material base and institutional superstructure. Accordingly, he was concerned with the effects of a transnational capitalist system – the material base – on superstructural social institutions of several kinds, including states and firms, all of which moved roughly in parallel but each of which was to be regarded as one facet of a single phenomenon. He unhelpfully chose to call this phenomenon imperialism, which was to put most of his English-speaking critics in mind of the European conquest of colonies in Africa and Asia. In Lenin's analogy, the several facets of imperialism included the process of division of territory among the Great Powers and a parallel division of world markets among oligopolistic firms. The one did not *cause* the other. Inadequate though it certainly was in its gross understatement of the productive potential of capitalism, Lenin's theory was a lucid and systemic analysis.

The predominantly European and liberal story that has been told thus far came to exert an extraordinary influence on United States foreign policy. US policy-makers of the 1940s promoted economic multilateralism through macroeconomic management of each national economy. This included the manipulation of taxation, government spending, and money supply, backed up by the Bretton Woods IFIs. These policies were regarded as ways of avoiding war by stabilizing global capitalism. This justificatory narrative rested on the conviction that protectionism and economic nationalism had led to global economic crisis and contributed to Great Power wars, while capitalism and liberal democracy, by contrast, were mutually supportive objectives. These beliefs were fostered by liberal interpretations of European history from the Industrial Revolution, through the long peace of the mid-nineteenth century, to the world wars of the twentieth century, and the catastrophic financial crisis and subsequent global depression of the 1930s. This lamentable European story had brought the world to war, and its repetition was to be avoided at all costs.

In these readings of history the emphasis fell squarely on certain aspects of classical liberalism while others were neglected. This was because abstracting economy and polity from social relations overcame Marxist emphasis on changing material culture. The effect of that changing culture was evident in an ever-increasing scale of bureaucratic organization across states, firms, and organized religions. While economic liberalism argued for states to remain as small as possible and idolized the self-made entrepreneur, liberal democracy argued for increasing provision of welfare and large firms became more and more dominant. State spending accounted for an ever larger share of GDP, even in the USA, while markets became ever more concentrated. Public and private bureaucracies flourished throughout the superstructure of the capitalist system.

Classical liberals had campaigned for the removal of impediments to trade, including tariff and non-tariff barriers; the GATT and the more recent WTO have been faithful to that memory. But liberals had also campaigned against monopolies, and in this they have been notably less successful. By the end of the eighteenth century the London-based East India Company ruled much of India directly or indirectly and had exclusive control over trade between its vast territories and the British Isles. At home, the company had gained such sway in the British legislature as to constitute a state within the state. Reform brought the company to heel early in the nineteenth century, reducing territorial monopoly and ushering in a period in which relatively small-scale partnerships predominated.

Increasingly, the financial insecurity and impermanence of partnership proved inadequate when faced with the challenge of new, capital-hungry technologies. Partnership generally entailed each member of a company staking his or her entire fortune.

This gave good assurance to those with whom a merchant firm did business that they would get what was owing to them in the event of loss. However, it depended on partners knowing and trusting one another, and being right to do so, and was therefore a system that could not safely be extended beyond a relatively small number of investors. Capitalists wanting to limit the financial liability of the large number of investors needed to fund a canal, a bank, or any other capital-intensive project, generally had to secure specific legislation for their project up to the middle of the nineteenth century. This could be very expensive, and created a serious barrier to market entry and economic growth.

The reason that general limited liability by a simple and cheap process of registration had been widely conceded by the second half of the nineteenth century was that more and more new technologies − expensive to set up but profitable in the long run − were putting the cost of initial investment beyond groups of entrepreneurs personally known to one another. In a public company with thousands or tens of thousands of investors, each individual could not be expected to risk total loss should a board of directors fail to manage it competently. Only by limiting liability to the nominal value of the shares owned by each individual could entrepreneurs hope to raise the massive amounts needed for railways, submarine telegraph cables, international retail banks, or fleets of steamships. Often, investors bought shares with a high nominal value, but were at first required to pay only part of this amount: a first call. Leaving a percentage of the share capital uncalled provided a reserve against which to borrow, or to be called up if times got rough or a major expansion was needed. It also allowed limited companies to reassure those with whom they dealt of their ability to meet their obligations.

The system spread rapidly throughout Europe and the Americas and beyond, mobilizing the savings of a rising middle class and making possible the exploitation of a wave of capital-hungry technologies known collectively as the Second Industrial Revolution. These included processes and innovations as diverse as chrome tanning of leather, cyanidation of gold ores, the compound marine steam engine, and the Bessemer steel production process. It was a brilliant system, but it had two great flaws. The first snag was nicely captured by Stephen Williamson, a Scots merchant on the Pacific coast around the time of the 1862 British Companies Act. Who would want to deal with people who did not stand to lose heavily if they were not straight? Limited liability, the Scot thundered, 'was un-English and [would] lead to mischief'. Yet before long his own firm had moved into company promotion and Williamson himself was shifting more and more of his personal fortune into publicly traded shares in limited liability companies.

The second weakness of the system was that there was practically no limit to the size to which a limited liability company could grow. The outcome was generally that while investors risked little, typical firm size in transport, finance, and global trading increased, and many smaller producers found themselves squeezed. Just as farmers today face immensely powerful buyers from the major supermarkets, so farmers in the USA by the 1880s generally had access to the lines of only one railroad company and the storage facilities of only one grain merchant. They had no option but to accept rates and prices that often appeared unfair to them. The populism that resulted was never anti-capitalist, but it was certainly angry, contemptuous of big business, and strong enough to mount a credible presidential challenge in the election of 1896.

The outcome was the anti-trust movement, the US name for what Europeans call competition policy. But the effect of national competition policies, and of EU collective policy, has often been simply to lead large corporations to look to other jurisdictions once they reach a position of near-dominance at home. At the end of the 1980s, faced with insurmountable legal obstacles to further acquisitions in its home market, British sugar giant Tate & Lyle opted instead for purchases in Australia, Canada, continental Europe, and the USA, simultaneously adding corn syrup and other sweeteners to its traditional sugar products. Together with vastly improved logistical systems, national anti-trust policies have led to the substitution of global oligopolies for national ones, leaving many firms with increased autonomy from any single state. The economic outcome of this process of scarcely constrained growth has been a global economy increasingly dominated by large firms. The sociological outcome has been the formation of a global capitalist class more cosmopolitan than the political elites that support it, who – in turn – are more cosmopolitan in outlook than the political communities they represent. It is unhelpful to long, nostalgically, for the representatives of electorates, organized labour, regions, and corporations to be able to convene at national level to thrash out their differences. Instead, all concerned are having to adapt to more dispersed and unpredictable political geographies.

This might matter less had the sophistication of corporate governance kept pace with that of business administration and management, but inventive corporate structures have in some instances allowed families to retain nominal control of empires that exceed their managerial competence, as with the media conglomerate of the Murdoch family. More usually, substantial holdings are held by institutional investors such as pension funds, or by other corporations. This means that corporate value and values, while ultimately based in performance, are modulated by credit rating agencies, financial journalists, gurus, and bloggers. These in their turn are about as accessible to workers, individual shareholders, and consumers as are the processes of government in mature liberal democracies to ordinary voters. The outcome has been a global shift to close collusion between corporate and political elites, greater income inequality, and the emergence of an underclass: in all, a practical negation of the spirit of individual emancipation that stands at the origin of liberalism.

Nationalist Responses to Liberalism

The first impulse of liberalism is not to regulate at all. At its inception the great motto was *Laissez faire, laisser aller*, which may be roughly translated as 'Let people do what they please and go where they please'. Coined by French economists in the eighteenth century, this phrase was soon adopted by anglophone liberals. But from the late nineteenth century forms of compensatory liberalism developed, in which states intervened in the economy to counter perceived shortcomings of the liberal project. Within their own territories this meant the creation of welfare systems to combat poverty, which was regarded as a recruiting agent for extremist political parties. Abroad, it took the form of international co-operation under US leadership to create a stable and prosperous world calculated to avoid any repeat of the sequence from global economic crisis, through nationalist response, to war.

By the middle of the twentieth century the policies associated with this late form of liberalism were, in reality, not so very different from those fostered by the self-consciously anti-liberal tradition that can be traced from the early decades of independence in the USA, through the process of economic integration that prefigured German unification, to the pooled economic nationalisms of the Global South. Most American states had retained high tariffs following independence for lack of other convenient sources of revenue. The USA went further, using its tariff to shield industry from global competition. Alexander Hamilton (1755 or 1757–1804) was a prominent economic nationalist in the young North American confederation, and the first man to hold the office of Secretary of the Treasury, from 1789 to 1795. Hamilton favoured state intervention to promote business, including the use of high tariffs to protect infant manufacturing industries. His political influence waned following the 1800 presidential election, but his ideas, notably in the 1791 'Report on Manufactures', were to continue to influence US thought during economic downturns. The baton that fell when he died, in 1804, was taken up and ably carried by Henry Clay. Clay was the Kentucky lawyer who anticipated Mahatma Gandhi by more than a century when, in 1809, he proposed that members of the state legislature should wear homespun instead of imported British broadcloth. He went on, as a leading Whig, to advocate protectionist tariffs, state provision of physical infrastructure, and a national bank.

Friedrich List, a native of Württemberg who lived in the USA between 1825 and 1832, later maintained in his 1841 *National System of Political Economy* that only a large domestic market behind a protective tariff wall could hope to resist and ultimately match British strength in manufactured textiles and metal goods. His work helped justify the 1834–66 expansion of the German *zollverein* (customs union), much as Ricardo's had legitimized the practical free trade politics of Cobden. By the end of the century the industrial success and economic growth of Germany and the United States were being widely imitated. Governments throughout Europe and beyond responded to downturns in the business cycle by raising tariffs and assuring themselves of exclusive access to sources of strategic raw materials. These economic policies heightened international tension and contributed to the outbreak of war in 1914. The interwar period brought serious disruption to the world economy. After a brief boom in 1919–20, world prices of raw materials slumped. Well aware of Ricardo's theory of comparative advantage, independent states reliant on exports of grain, sugar, and other bulk commodities jibed at the tendency of international trade to perpetuate existing patterns of production and pointed out that while Ricardo had established that all would gain from free trade, he had offered no guarantee of equal *distribution* of the gains.

A particularly influential formulation of these objections was developed by the Argentine economist Raúl Prebisch (1901–86), and provided the ideological rationale for nationalistic economic policies and calls for international reform in many parts of the Global South. Prebisch argued that the relative prices of exports from and imports to countries that predominantly exported primary products would deteriorate over time. The reason these terms of trade would move against primary exporters was that each household would spend more on manufactured goods and services and a diminishing proportion of income on housing and foodstuffs as incomes rose. This assumption, often referred to as Engel's law, after German economist Ernst Engel (1821–96), implied that demand for tea or cereals would slacken while demand for sewing machines and automobiles was still rising relatively fast, and prices would reflect this progressive shift in demand. Worse, industrial firms were generally much larger than the typical agro-industrial firm at the time and produced more specialized goods. Labour organization was also much more advanced in the industrialized countries. There, the unions were able to restrict access to skilled trades and bid up wages. In the Argentine countryside, by contrast, labour organization was weak, and an unlimited supply of local and immigrant unskilled labour kept wages low. The effect of these differential levels of organization and market power amplified the effect of Engel's law.

From this argument about the terms of trade it followed that reliance on the export of primary commodities was a poor long-term national strategy. The remedy was for the state to intervene to counteract the organizational and negotiating strengths of those firms and countries that imported primary goods while also promoting industries which would produce substitutes for the ever more costly imports of machinery and consumer goods from Europe and the USA. The first objective was to be achieved by state-sponsored international co-operation between exporters of non-perishable commodities, as had already been tried with sugar and coffee. This was expected to stabilize prices by controlling supply and stockpiling surpluses. A second device was the creation of state-owned national corporations, notably in the petroleum industry, to counter the power of the so-called Seven Sisters – privately owned transnational oil giants based in Britain, the Netherlands, and the USA. Between them these giant firms controlled more than eighty percent of the world's oil reserves in 1973. A third strand of policy was the erection of high tariffs around selected industries to encourage local enterprise or, just as often, to force transnational corporations to leap over the tariff wall and manufacture locally in order to avoid loss of global market share. Finally, Prebisch encouraged regional integration through abandonment of tariffs within free trade areas or customs unions in order to create larger domestic markets capable of sustaining advanced manufacturing industries. In a free trade area (FTA) each country maintains its own tariff against imports from the rest of the world; goods substantially produced in any member state move freely across frontiers, but rules of origin prevent the member with the lowest external tariff from being used as a back door to the rest of the FTA. In a customs union, the members establish a common external tariff, obviating the need for rules of origin.

This bundle of policies was generally known as Import Substituting Industrialization (ISI). Coupled with some version of macroeconomic management, it swept across Latin America from the 1930s onwards and informed the collective nationalism of the Global South, as decolonization gained pace after the Second World War. The appointment of Prebisch as Secretary of the UN Commission for Latin America in 1948 and subsequently, in 1964, as founding Secretary General of UNCTAD helped spread the word.

The point of reviewing the ideas on which the North–South dialogue was based – neo-liberalism on the one hand and Prebisch's structuralism on the other – is to expose an ideological battle every bit as important and entrenched as those between democracy and authoritarianism or capitalism and communism. Prebisch was no Left-winger, and the kinds of nationalist policies he advocated, while often seen as indistinguishable from those of more radical socialists or communists by officials in the US State Department, assumed the possibility of an equitable global capitalist economy and owed more to US populism than to European Marxist thought. It is otherwise hard to see why his policies appealed to governments of the Right and to military regimes, as well as to Left-nationalists, over such a long period. But the alliance of Left and Right was fragile, and Latin American Marxists were attacking the ISI model by the 1960s, alarmed by the willingness of some of their number to work in coalition with centrist parties such as the Chilean Christian Democrats. They maintained that equalization of power between the industrialized core of the world economy and its periphery could not be achieved. Reformist policies were accordingly bankrupt. It was not that the periphery was lagging behind and needed to catch up, but that the mounting prosperity of the core was premised on a progressive impoverishment or underdevelopment of the periphery.

Accepting a good deal of what Prebisch had had to say about unequal trade, writers of the dependency school (*dependentistas* in Spanish) added a class argument which, they felt, explained the impossibility of reform and the necessity of armed revolution. The pattern of development inflicted by the capitalist core on the Global South had distorted its class structure, strengthening the position of traditional landed groups, equivalent to the European aristocracy, while hampering the development of national bourgeoisies, many of whose sources of income were dominated by foreign capitalists, who owned much of the commercial and physical infrastructure of the modern sector in peripheral countries. The social composition of the state therefore made effective reform along the lines proposed by Prebisch impossible.

Active and widely read in the 1960s, the *dependentistas* ran into trouble from two sources in the 1970s. The first was criticism from social scientists in the USA who challenged the neo-Marxists to formulate their views as a testable theory. The social scientists relied on a distinction drawn by the Austrian philosopher of science, Karl Popper, between theories proper, which must be able to survive tests aimed at proving them false, and ideologies that resisted expression in testable form. This was appropriate, since Popper had written with the precise intention of driving a wedge between the claims of Marxism and other secular creeds to scientific status, and the pursuit of those he regarded as true sciences, including physics, chemistry, and astronomy.

Of more urgent and local political importance was a second criticism, rooted in the embarrassing fact that a number of peripheral countries that ought to have been stagnating were in fact growing apace, including Brazil, Mexico, and South Korea. Predictions made only a few years before had turned out to be inaccurate. The manner in which this was dealt with precisely illustrates the source of the first, more academic objection. Marx famously said that the bourgeoisie was the executive committee of the state. But no executive committee simply does what the majority of members want it to. Its responsibility is to take an overview and devise policies in the general and long-term interest of the organization in question. The concept of the relative autonomy of the state was born. The reason over-powerful landed classes in peripheral countries did not automatically stymie reform, producing stagnation and revolution, was that the state itself had sufficient autonomy to compensate for the weakness of the industrial bourgeoisie and act on the advice of Giuseppe di Lampedusa's Sicilian prince: 'There'll have to be changes if things are to stay as they are.' Cheated of their prey by this deft move, Northern social scientists began to wonder whether dependency *theory*, as they insisted on calling it, was falsifiable at all. If it was not, it surely followed that it was nothing more than ideology, and therefore to be dismissed.

These arguments were not merely academic. The question of whether economic growth was best achieved by reform or revolution lay at the heart of contemporary politics and Cold War superpower rivalry. Fidel Castro had taken power in Cuba in 1959 and turned decisively to Moscow in 1961. Che Guevara (1928–67) was fighting in Bolivia in 1966–67. Urban guerrillas were active not just in the southern cone of South America but also in Germany, Ireland, Italy, and Spain. Successive US administrations were growing more and more concerned as the South gained momentum in myriad forums, from UNCTAD through UNCLOS.

What finally blew apart the ISI strategy and marked the beginning of the end for the first phase of the North–South dialogue was neither criticism from the Left nor theoretical weakness as such. Instead, a combination of the practical consequences of a spike in interest rates, falling prices for primary commodities, and – above all – United States resumption of Cold War rivalry after a decade of uncertainty drew this phase of economic nationalism to a close. Yet the model had been living on borrowed time even before these events, beset by its own internal contradictions. These were three. Very few domestic markets were big enough to allow advanced manufacturing industries to operate at full capacity. In many countries this meant, for example, that the cost of each automobile coming off an assembly line was higher than it would have been had the assembly plant been working at or near its planned level of output. The tariff was protecting infant industries that could never grow up.

The second problem was negative rates of effective protection for globally competitive sectors. Protectionism helps producers if it keeps out products that compete with theirs in the domestic market. They are able to sell their goods above world prices, gaining from a positive rate of protection. But the policy has precisely the reverse effect on firms that depend on those artificially expensive goods as inputs. They suffer a negative rate of protection. If, as a farmer, you have no choice but to buy tractors and fertilizers at artificially high local prices because those industries receive positive protection, your own competitiveness in global markets is clearly reduced because farmers in other countries are buying these inputs at lower world prices. The third problem was that stabilization of commodity prices by exporter cartels stimulated the entry of new suppliers from outside the cartel (and cheating by those within) and was ultimately self-defeating.

Besides, the distinction between exporters of primary products and exporters of manufactures had always been a weak link. The USA exported both. Also, many primary commodities, notably metals, are not subject to Engel's law; demand for them is a function of demand for manufactured goods, which continues to grow faster than demand for foodstuffs. Finally, the shift of manufacturing from the old core of the world economy into East Asia, coupled with the rise of TNCs based outside North America and Western Europe, has meant that patterns of global production and divisions between North and South are now much less clear than they were a generation ago. These developments invalidated the theoretical base of twentieth-century economic nationalism. The neo-liberal conditions set by the IMF, the World Bank, and global TNCs in exchange for loans and investment demolished the institutions that had been based on that theory.

The Sociological Base of the World Economy

The general argument of this chapter has been that the 1980s witnessed a qualitative change in the global economy. Starting from the 1982 debt crisis and culminating in the unification of

Germany in 1990 and the break-up of the Soviet Union the following year, this short period saw an emphatic rejection of central planning and constraints on international trade and investment, whether communist or nationalist. The emergence of truly global TNCs and a cosmopolitan class of capitalists and senior executives rendered the political elites of all but the most powerful states almost parochial by contrast, their performance wide open to the judgement of global markets. Both the Euro and the US dollar felt the hand of these markets on their collar in the northern-hemisphere summer of 2011.

In short, the leading capitalists at the start of the twenty-first century are no longer members of national bourgeoisies, lobbying imperial states, as was true up to the 1970s. Accordingly policy proposals grounded in past ideologies have lost their sociological footing, whether the appeal is to the *laissez faire* liberalism of Richard Cobden, the managed capitalism of English economist John Maynard Keynes, or the economic nationalism of Raúl Prebisch. Class struggle between bourgeoisie and aristocracy or proletariat and bourgeoisie, as much a feature of nineteenth-century liberal thought as of Marxism, no longer makes sense. Far fewer see this as the motor of a progressive history; rather more, perhaps, now pin their hopes on divine providence. Francis Fukuyama famously announced that 1989 marked the end of history, and has since been mocked for it. But his central claim was that events would continue to occur but could no longer be made sense of by resort to grand narratives such as those of liberalism and Marxism. Here, surely, he was right. Recent wars, by contrast with the Spanish Civil War of 1936–39, the Second World War, or the Korean War, have been difficult to regard as clashes of high principle or decisive strategic moment. Revolutions take place, as in Egypt in the spring of 2011, but their meaning remains unclear.

Neo-liberalism is therefore economistic: it relies entirely on the rationality of utility-maximizing individuals and free markets, without providing anything resembling the sociological explanations or moral justifications of classical liberalism. This incoherence is especially evident in current thought about the mass of semi-skilled and modestly paid workers on whom the whole structure ultimately relies.

The rise of manufacturing following the economic reforms of the 1980s has only been possible because of massive flows of people from rural areas to the cities, most of all in China, and the concurrent relocation of manufacturing to countries with tight control of labour and restricted rights. The number of internal migrants in China, estimated at thirty million in 1989, had risen to more than 140 million by 2008 and was perhaps as high as 250 million three years later. This is a little more than twenty percent of the entire population and exceeds estimates of the manufacturing labour force. Yet it is a plausible figure, since many of the migrants may be assumed to be active in unrecorded service activities. It is also proportionate to the level of internal migration in the then United Kingdom of Britain and Ireland at the height of the First Industrial Revolution. But whereas that process rocked the British state, the government of China, like those of India and Brazil, appeared to be managing the process with greater ease, their new middle-classes preoccupied with consumption and their workers cowed and disorganized. The conditions for class solidarity and action at national level hardly exist, and it is merely nostalgic to seek them. Instead, the characteristic contemporary forms of action are mercurial, rapidly organized, using social networking sites and mobile phones, often centring on single issues, their leaders open to co-option by patient states and repression by resolutely brutal ones.

4
Armed conflict

When differences run deep and negotiations fail, violence sometimes seems the only way to resolve conflict. When those who resort to the use of force command large organized groups, we call it war. War between modern states was a principal stimulus for systematic study of international relations in the twentieth century; thoughts about how to conduct, avert, and regulate conventional wars has been at the heart of IR from the start. But not much can be said with precision about war unless it is clear what counts as a war and what does not.

That phrase, 'conventional war', fuses two quite distinct ideas. The first is war between well-constituted states. The second is a struggle between and more or less evenly matched forces, each using similar tactics and weapons. By this definition, the War on Terror waged by the USA and its allies after the 9/11 bombings of 2001 was no more a proper war than recent gang warfare in Mexico, because al-Qaeda is not a state, the forces in play are highly asymmetrical, and the means employed by the two sides very different. But extension of the term 'war' to cover all and any large-scale manifestations of public violence recovers earlier practice, which was to distinguish between public and private wars: the first between sovereign states and the second between lesser authorities or between a state and a non-state actor.

	Duration	Principal belligerents	Battle deaths (approximate)
First Kashmir War	1947–48	India, Pakistan	3,000–4,000
Arab–Israeli War	1948–49	Egypt, Syria, Lebanon, Jordan, Iraq, Israel	12,000–19,000
Korean War	1950–53	S. Korea, N. Korea, China (PRC), USA	350,000–2,000,000
Offshore Islands War	1954–55	China (PRC) and Taiwan (ROC)	n/a
Sinai War	1956	Israel, Egypt, Britain, France	1,800–3,800
Soviet invasion of Hungary	1956	Hungary, USSR	3,200
Ifni War	1957–58	Spain, Morocco	8,300
Taiwan Straits War	1958	China (PRC) and Taiwan (ROC)	n/a
War in Assam	1962	China (PRC) and India	2,000
Vietnam War, phase 2	1965–75	N. Vietnam, S. Vietnam, USA, S. Korea	1,400,000
Second Kashmir War	1965	India and Pakistan	6,800
Six Day War	1967	Israel, Egypt, Syria, Iraq, Jordan	14,000–23,000

	Duration	Principal belligerents	Battle deaths (approximate)
Second Laoatian War, phase 2	1968–73	Vietnam, USA, Laos, Thailand	See Vietnam War
War of Attrition	1969–70	Israel, Egypt, USSR	4,000+
Football War	1969	El Salvador, Honduras	Fewer than 3,000
War of the Communist Coalition	1970–71	Cambodia, North Vietnam, South Vietnam, USA	?
War for Bangladesh	1971	India, Pakistan, Bangladesh	40,000
Yom Kippur War	1973	Israel, Egypt, Syria, Iraq, Jordan	10,000–20,000
Turco-Cypriot War	1974	Turkey, Cyprus	1,200–2,300
War over Angola	1975–76	Angola, Cuba, South Africa, USA, USSR	n/a
Second Ogaden War, phase 2	1977–78	Ethipoia, Soalia, S. Yemen, Cuba, USSR	13,000
Vietnamese–Cambodian Border War	1977–79	Vietnam, Cambodia	30,000
Ugandan–Tanzanian War	1978–79	Uganda, Libya, Tanzania	3,000
Iran–Iraq War	1980–88	Iran, Iraq	600,000

	Duration	Principal belligerents	Battle deaths (approximate)
Falklands War	1982	Argentina, Britain	1,000
War over Lebanon	1982	Israel, Suria, Lebanon	28,000
War over the Aouzou Strip	1986–87	Libya, Chad	8,500
Sino-Vietnamese Border War	1987	China (PRC) and Vietnam	37,000
Gulf War	1990–91	Kuwait, Iraq, USA, Britain, etc.	20,000–35,000
Azeri–Armenian War	1993–94	Azerbaijan, Armenia	30,000–35,000
Cenepa Valley War	1995	Ecuador, Peru	500
Badme Border War	1998–2000	Eritrea, Ethiopia	53,000
War for Kosovo	1999	Yugoslavia/ Serbia, Albania, NATO	2,500
Kargil War	1999	India, Pakistan	1,000–4,500
Invasion of Afghanistan	2001	Afghan factions, NATO (USA, etc.)	n/a
Invasion of Iraq	2003	Iraq, USA, and allies	8,000–45,000

Figure 7 Inter-state wars since 1945
Source: Correlates of War 2010 list at http://www.correlatesofwar.org.

War, in this broad sense, has been endemic since the beginning of history. It has certainly been frequent in recent times. Various estimates have been attempted for different time spans. One authoritative list of conventional wars since 1945 is offered in Figure 7. The most remarkable feature of this list is the absence of direct wars between major powers. The second is that it includes some wars widely familiar to US and European publics and others few will have heard of. Up to 1991 proxy wars between client states of the USA and the Soviet Union commanded the attention of global media because of their relevance to superpower strategic rivalry and they accordingly dominated public perceptions in the West. Western reliance on oil and the sustained attachment of the USA to Israel have meant that wars between Israel and its neighbours in 1948, 1956, 1967, and 1973 received especially close scrutiny, as did those between Iraq and its neighbours (1980–88, 1990–91). The first of these, between Iraq and Iran, is perhaps the clearest recent example of a sustained conventional war. Proximity and, later, flows of migrants and direct engagement of Western troops account for European and US concern over the Balkan wars of the 1990s.

The Iran–Iraq War, 1980–88

Hoping to take advantage of Iranian disarray following the 1978–79 Islamic Revolution and the overthrow of the Shah, Iraqi leader Saddam Hussein invaded Iran in 1980. His aim was to establish Iraq as the leading power in the Persian Gulf by resolving longstanding disputes about the Arab-populated south-western Khuzestan province of Iran and the Shatt al Arab channel along which Iranian oil reached the high seas.

Traditional animosities had been inflamed following the 1979 appeal by Iranian leader Ayatollah Khomeini for Iraqi Shia Moslems to overthrow the ostensibly secular Sunni regime in Iraq. Iraq attacked without warning. The war was initially fought in a quite conventional manner, using sophisticated weapons platforms on land, at sea, and in the air. In one early battle as many as 150 tanks were lost by the opposing armies. As early as 1982 Iran had made good its initial territorial losses and Iraq was forced into a defensive posture.

The next six years were costly, brutal, yet inconclusive. Both sides resorted to unconventional tactics. Iran took advantage of revolutionary zeal to launch sacrificial 'human waves' consisting of poorly armed infantry unsupported by artillery or air power. Iraq resorted to the use of chemical weapons, banned by international law, and to city bombing and attacks on civilian public transport. Echoing the two world wars of the twentieth century in its use of massed infantry, chemical weapons, and heavily armoured vehicles, and the level of casualties, the direct cost of the war exceeded $1 trillion and 600,000 or more died in battle. It has been thought of by optimists as the last Fordist war, employing the techniques of industrial mass production on the battlefield.

It is not hard to see why wars in which Western troops have been actively engaged should have commanded most attention at home. These include Korea (1950–53), Suez (1956), South-East Asia (a complex struggle in effect lasting from 1945 to 1979), Kuwait (1991), Afghanistan (2001–), and Iraq (2003–10). More limited and local attention has been devoted to engagements of national troops in the disentanglement of European states from their former dependencies, occasional forays of the United States into the Caribbean Basin, such as the Dominican Republic intervention of 1964, or UN peacekeeping operations of which there have been more than sixty since 1945.

By contrast, vastly more destructive conflicts elsewhere have received little coverage. In part this has been because they had little strategic significance for major powers. A second reason for obscurity has been that many such conflicts have consisted in the attempts of fragile states to quell long-running insurrections, easily dismissed as civil wars, even when they spill over state frontiers or are fought between distinct ethnic groups. What stands out most of all is the neglect, by Western publics and mass media, of ongoing wars in sub-Saharan Africa that together have claimed the lives of many millions. The most deadly of these is the war in the Congo Basin, but at least ten other conflicts in Africa since independence have resulted in more than 100,000 deaths, direct and indirect, and together they account for close to five million deaths. Not quite fitting the standard twentieth-century definition of conventional war, they have been marginalized by mass media and scholars alike and are notable for their absence from Figure 7.

War in the Congo Basin

If indirect casualties resulting from disease and famine are included, the most destructive conflict since the end of the Cold War has been the complex sequence of interconnected struggles in the Congo Basin. Estimates of the number of violent deaths, at around 300,000, seem small only by comparison with the appalling total of 5.4 million when indirect casualties from disease and starvation are included. These figures rise if the precursors to the main conflict are included.

By the late 1980s violence in Rwanda had led many from the economically dominant Tutsi minority to seek refuge in neighbouring Uganda or Zaire (known as the Democratic Republic of Congo – DRC – from 1997). In 1990 the Tutsi diaspora launched an armed campaign to regain their land and rights in Rwanda, and a settlement was reached in August 1993. Hutu leaders who felt too much had been conceded organized and armed an extensive militia, intent on eliminating the Tutsis once and for all. The death of the Hutu presidents of Rwanda and neighbouring Burundi, when their plane was shot down in April 1994, triggered a massacre in which somewhere between 500,000 and 800,000 died.

Many of those responsible later fled to the DRC, where armed groups opposed to the Ugandan government had also sought refuge, and this provided the pretext for an invasion of the DRC by Rwanda and Uganda in 1998. Troops from Angola, Namibia, and Zimbabwe rallied to defend the DRC in a war that ended, formally, in 2003, though fighting has continued in eastern parts of the country, where rape and the use of child soldiers are commonplace. At the height of the conflict, troops from at least eight African countries were involved in hostilities on DRC territory, but the war was virtually ignored by Western media, and, when reported at all, was presented as an anarchic and meaningless *intra*-state struggle between ethnic groups, made possible by state failure.

One of the many reasons that Western media consistently devoted less attention to events in the DRC than to the Iran–Iraq War, and less to that gruelling struggle than to Arab–Israeli skirmishing, is that these three conflicts are of ascending strategic importance to Western governments and publics. In general, those in the West notice wars in countries they once ruled and where their own language is spoken. Figures for the coverage of the first two years of the African 'World War' in Central Africa show the highest level of media interest in Belgium, former colonial master of the DRC, and the lowest on US-based CNN, with *Le Monde*, a leading French daily newspaper, midway between the two. People care more about conflicts that directly affect their daily lives or those of their countrymen and women. So ongoing violence between government troops, guerrillas, and vigilante militias in Colombia has caught the attention of Western media mainly because US military aid and advisers have been involved, and because the country is a major supplier of cocaine to the USA. They care most of all when their own troops are at risk and the war is judged a matter of national security.

How Many Wars?

The reason many scholars have tried to classify and list wars has been their belief that to examine them systematically – determining their frequency, distribution, and causes – may help prevent them in future. Writing in 1972, US political scientists J.

David Singer and Melvin Small insisted that 'until war has been systematically described, it cannot be adequately understood, and with such understanding comes the first meaningful possibility of controlling it, eliminating it, or finding less reprehensible substitutes for it'.

The great variety of wars means that this aspiration is not easily satisfied. Positivist social scientists try to apply the methods of the natural sciences to social phenomena. This project requires reliable descriptive terms. Unfortunately description of society is not straightforward. Sodium is sodium whether we like it or not, and will always respond the same way to an established set of tests. Concepts such as democracy, state, and war are much less stable. Their meanings are conventional – determined by mutual agreement; and that agreement is not always present. Heated debate about gay marriage is not entirely a consequence of homophobia; it stems in part from disagreements about the very nature of marriage. So if the intention is to engage in scientific analysis of war, using statistical methods, firm decisions must be taken at the outset about classification and the meanings of key terms. That way the shifting meaning of war can be stabilized to the point where its definition is almost as reliable as that of sodium. Only then can the data be sorted or coded consistently. The problem besetting positivist social science is that theoretical assumptions often slip unnoticed into purportedly neutral descriptive terms that are then used to state a theory. The supposedly raw empirical observations that the theory claims to organize are already coloured by theory.

This difficulty has been understood but not wholly resolved by those involved in the most sustained modern attempt to understand war using inductive reasoning and statistical analysis. Inductive reasoning works from the bottom up, looking for correlations in the natural or social world and then proposing testable theoretical explanations that might account for observed regularities. The Correlates of War (CoW) project, founded by J. David Singer in 1963 at the University of Michigan, has developed data sets relating to armed conflicts since 1816, lately distinguishing between inter-state, intra-state, non-state, and extra-state conflicts. The first category includes wars fought between recognized states and until recently was the major focus of attention by scholars associated with the project. The second group consists of wars fought between groups within a state, commonly called civil wars. Third come non-state wars, fought between entities which are not states. Finally, extra-state wars are fought between states and non-state entities beyond their frontiers. The project has also systematically collected data about possible causes of war such as alliances, arms racing, escalation, regime type, and the distribution of power in the inter-state system.

It is worth taking a close look at the original CoW definition of inter-state war. The first surprise is that the hugely destructive and enduring war in the Congo Basin, described in the previous section, is absent from the CoW list of inter-state wars in Figure 7. This is because it does not meet the project's criteria. Even though it is *named* as 'Africa's World War of 1998–2002' it is *classified* as an intra-state war.

To count as a war, an armed conflict had to show sustained hostilities between effective forces resulting in at least 1,000 battle deaths of military personnel. To count as an inter-state war, fighting should be between and not within 'nations' (sic), defined as states consisting of organized sovereign polities with a population of 500,000 or more, and diplomatic missions from Britain and France (which seemed arbitrary to many). The initial objective was to isolate wars between modern states, since it was preventing this kind of conflict that was the most urgent concern of the research project.

The object of the minimum of 1,000 battle deaths was to exclude skirmishes, sporadic exchanges of fire across disputed frontiers, and other relatively small clashes of arms. The disagreements that give rise to such incidents are often referred to, collectively, as militarized inter-state disputes (MIDs). In March 2008 Colombia attacked a unit of the Fuerzas Armadas de la Revolución Colombiana (FARC) that had taken refuge just inside Ecuador. Venezuela sided with an outraged Ecuador and sent tanks to the Colombian border. A typical MID, this incident hit the headlines for a day or two, but was never likely to escalate. The question left hanging by the exclusion of such incidents from the lists of wars is whether they may have acted as substitutes for full-blown warfare in Latin America, in which case careful analysis of them, and of the skills required to sustain brinkmanship of this kind, might be thought valuable.

Indeed, any restriction makes a difference to what can be done with the resultant data set. Excluding the kinds of coercive diplomacy and military intervention once routinely practiced by the USA in Central America and the Caribbean throughout the twentieth century prejudices any investigation that might later be undertaken, for example, into the question of whether democracies or Great Powers are more or less belligerent than other kinds of states.

US interventions in Central America and the Caribbean

Interventions in which US troops or agents were the leading element:

1961	Cuba
1965	Dominican Republic
1983	Granada
1989	Panama

Changes of government by force in which the USA was implicated:

1954	Guatemala
1960	Guatemala
1961	Ecuador
1963	Dominican Republic
1973	Chile

Next comes the requirement that an armed conflict must be between and not within 'nations' to count as a war. The primary purpose of this rule was to bracket civil wars, wars of secession (at least if they are unsuccessful), and colonial wars; the objective of the CoW has been to focus on wars between polities *as defined by the founders of the project*. But a variety of political forms have existed, even in relatively recent times. It would be absurd to claim that the temporal authority of the Holy Roman Emperor meant that conflicts between states within the empire were not really wars, whereas conflicts between the Emperor's forces and the expeditionary forces of Denmark, France, and Sweden were. Picking apart the Thirty Years War (1618–48) to determine which bits were inter-state and which merely intra-state would be a methodological nightmare and a historical absurdity.

This particular example lies outside the post-1815 time-frame of the CoW project, but it can be plausibly argued that the Confederate states in nineteenth-century North America had a right to secede because their sovereignty had not been fully dissolved into the Union, and that the American *Civil* War was so named by the victors as one mark of their victory. There are those who still prefer to call it the War Between the States. Nor does it seem immediately obvious that polities that became protectorates of the British Crown in the nineteenth century thereby became subordinate elements of a single British imperial state and lost the right to wage war against it. Quite the contrary: the ostensible, and often the initial, object of protectorate status, was precisely to preserve the distinct identity of such polities. That was how the Dutch-speaking Afrikaaners of the Transvaal and the Orange Free State understood their relationship with the British, and neither party hesitated to refer to the two conflicts they fought to resolve their differences as wars. In the second of these (1899–1902) the Empire committed more than a quarter of a million troops. This was no small war, and when CoW investigators classed two of the belligerents as non-systemic and excluded the conflict from the list of inter-state wars they were, in effect, siding with the victors on the main point at issue, which was whether or not the two Afrikaaner states had remained sovereign after signing the 1884 London Convention.

Finally, insistence on diplomatic recognition rules out the many wars fought by Argentina, Chile, and the United States against indigenous tribes or confederations encountered in the course of their territorial expansion and those between Britain and populous and organized independent South Asian states such as the Mahrattas (1817–18), Burma (1823–26), Afghanistan (1838–42 and 1878–80), Sindh (1842–43), and the Sikh kingdom of Lahore (1845–46 and 1848–49).

Insistence on minimum population and diplomatic recognition derived from an assumption that the behaviour of small pre-modern states was probably driven by reasons quite different from those motivating modern states. Researchers may also have assumed that too little was known about them for useful information to be gathered about possible causes of conflict such as alliance formation, past flare-ups, or arms build-ups. The first of these assumptions conflicts with the assumption of many political realists that self-reliance makes all polities functionally similar regardless of size or period; if we do not count as war the sustained hostilities between the Chilean state and the Mapuche or Araucanian peoples, who until the 1880s controlled extensive territories in modern Chile, then why should struggles between tiny Athens and Sparta, or fifteenth-century Italian micro-states, count? Social science should not and need not be at the mercy of the long-abandoned syllabi of European and North-American schools. Regarding the second assumption, we have already established that Africa, and the non-European world more generally, has much more ascertainable history than Europeans and North Americans were willing to concede half a century ago.

All these limitations, taken together, have ensured that any inferences drawn from the data for inter-state warfare have relevance to the particular kind of wars that the researchers are most concerned to avert. This is where the whole edifice comes crashing down. The fourfold classification developed by the CoW project can classify any war and can cope with changes of character as, for example, when an outside power intervenes in an intra-state war. It can accommodate al-Qaeda, the Taliban, the Colombian FARC, and the impromptu militias fighting to oust Gaddafi in Libya in the summer of 2011. But as Figure 7 demonstrates, it allocates to each of the four categories a set of conflicts having remarkably little in common with one another: some of them mere skirmishes, others apocalyptic contests. At the same time it ignores commonalities such as levels of destruction and styles of combat or ways of war. The reason for this is that the project was, from its inception, more concerned with the *politics* of war, conceived of as a deliberate act of state, than with its conduct or reality.

Statistical work of the sort attempted by CoW researchers requires careful coding of information. This in turn requires clear definitions, not just of war but of possible explanatory variables such as regime type or arms expenditure. Make the requirements too tight and the number of cases becomes too small to justify meaningful statistical analysis. Relax the criteria in order to secure a larger number of cases, or universe, and any statistically robust results may fail to apply to current cases because the world has changed since the research project was designed.

Ways of War

The original aim of the CoW project was to ascertain the causes of inter-state war, but even those conflicts captured by its standard definition have varied enormously in character from one decade to the next and, within the same conflict, from one theatre or phase to the next. Wars are complex and mercurial, comprising sieges, skirmishes, and raids. The archetypical expression of war is battle. Once upon a time the battlefield was just that: a field. By the end of 1914 a battle could be launched along a sector, several miles long, of a front extending several hundred miles. The defensive strength of such fronts was broken, twenty-five years later, by deep armoured thrusts that allowed defensive lines to be attacked from flank and rear until encircled, or kettled. The notion of a front more or less vanished as Russia rolled with German punches in 1942 and 1943 and long-range bombers pounded European cities deep behind the lines. Some wars require conscription; others are fought exclusively by professional volunteer forces. Some, such as the 1982 conflict between Britain and Argentina in the South Atlantic, take place far from major population centres; others have massive implications for civilians, whose sufferings may range from deprivation, mobilization, and bombardment at home to displacement, theft, rape, and massacre in areas of ground conflict.

There are two reasons why the character of war needs to be considered before turning to general explanations of the causes of war. It seems reasonable to suppose that the willingness of states to become involved in any particular conflict will reflect their expectation, however erroneous, of how long and costly it may turn out to be. A limited war comfortably distant from home is a very different undertaking from full-scale hostilities against a neighbouring state. More broadly, the attitude of a state towards involvement in a war may be influenced by a vision of the kind of war in which it is honourable or prudent to engage, and in which it has acquitted itself well in the past. Martial prowess is part of the national identity of some polities and not of others, and national identity may be reshaped by each new engagement.

Recent debate in the USA about ways of war illustrates this last point. From 1973 the standard view of characteristic US military strategy was influenced by military historian Russell Weigley (1930–2004). He had concluded that US military activity typically involved high-intensity conflicts away from US territory. A generation later, following the 9/11 attacks and the subsequent commitment of forces to Afghanistan and Iraq, US Air Force officer and historian John Grenier suggested that his predecessor had been influenced by what, at the time, were still recent military operations by US forces in Korea and Vietnam. He argued that the characteristic operations of the military forces that conquered North America disclosed a world in which irregular and unlimited warfare were typical. Little distinction had been made by either side between civilians and warriors, and no rules had been followed. Once the view of United States military culture was adjusted for this, aspects of contemporary military history that had at first seemed exceptional or aberrant began to fall into place. Those who accepted the orthodox view of United States military history had been disposed to dismiss the 1968 massacre of more than five hundred unarmed Vietnamese civilians at My Lai as an anomaly; likewise, the 2003–04 torture and abuse of Iraqi prisoners at the Abu Graib prison, near Baghdad. Instead, Grenier presented the first of these, an admitted atrocity by US troops in Vietnam, as 'a grim waypoint in the evolution of the American way of war'. Systematic violence against civilians, he argued, had been part of American warfare from the start.

Two conclusions follow. First, US military culture may turn out to have been less exceptional and more like that of other states than was once thought. Second, the claim that war is one of the institutions by which international society is regulated may be weakened. If it is bounded by custom and humanitarian law, fought with limited aims, and conducted with an eye to future political and military relations, war may resolve disputes between states and accommodate adjustments in their relative power. But it ceases to be an effective institution once a belligerent adopts revolutionary methods, employing weapons of mass destruction, killing non-combatants indiscriminately, or pursuing objectives that subvert international order, such as the elimination of opposing states.

War may also cease to be an institution of international society in the sense understood by Hedley Bull if the concentration of military power is such that the dominant power cannot be challenged by conventional means. Some feel that this has been the condition of the world since the collapse of the Soviet Union. There was much written in the 1990s about unipolarity and American Empire – a certain kind of military and possibly legal supremacy rather than territorial administration. In such circumstances the forces of the hegemonic or imperial state no longer act to maintain a balance of power but become a global police force, punishing any who dare to challenge the status quo and dominating the creation and interpretation of international law. The attack on Afghanistan by the USA and its allies following 9/11 can be read in this way, as a punitive expedition against al-Qaeda and its Taliban protectors. The 9/11 attack itself, conversely, can be seen as the perfect example of asymmetric warfare, achieving maximum publicity and inflicting maximum symbolic and material cost on an otherwise unassailable enemy by a spectacular breach of the conventions of war, which prohibit the deliberate targeting of non-combatants.

In a similar but more subtle and profound way, the first war of the US-led alliance against Iraq in 1991 was characterized by the French public intellectual Jean Baudrillard as a non-war. Baudrillard made much of the concept of hyper-reality. Representation had once been of real things in the world – the map representing territory, the mirror reflecting what stood before it – but now it more often represented a representation; for example, an image seen by those operating a weapons system merges with the image broadcast on a television news bulletin. The claim is not a grand metaphysical one: that there is no reality under all these representations. Rather it is that there has been a material change in the extent to which people experience life through representations, made possible by technological developments such as television, the internet, and social networks. Baudrillard noted a marked contrast between the surgical precision with which information was managed during the 1990–91 Kuwait crisis in order to create a clear justificatory narrative for military response against Iraq, and the wild profusion of interpretations that flourished in the aftermath of the high-intensity phase of the ensuing war. The real vanished into the virtual because of an excess of information, leaving so many traces that, as Baudrillard put it, 'generations of video-zombies ... will never cease reconstituting the event'. His practical response, as paraphrased by his translator, Paul Patton, was 'don't try, given this shower of information, to reconstitute the truth. It can't be done. Nor would it change the past.' History has become as impossible as war.

The central claim is not that mass media representations now smother reality so completely that there *is* no reality. Instead Baudrillard seems to have been making a more specific and plausible claim about social reality. Informational events such as the Gulf crisis are a feature of postmodern public life, and their claim to representation is extremely questionable. Baudrillard's thesis is not a general one, but relates to an important and growing class of events within which wars are prominent. The political moral is that 'since informational events are, by definition, always open to interpretation ... what matters is to control the production and meaning of information in a given context'.

In an age of immediate mass communication of images and generation of interpretations, the apparent privilege of participants, able to narrate events through services such as YouTube, Twitter, and Facebook, is neutralized in the editing rooms of news agencies and television channels. States, no longer in control of the mass media, struggle to shape public perceptions, as do their enemies. This was apparent in the war on terror that followed the 9/11 attacks of 2001. There are no terrorists; there are only people who adopt terrorism with more or less reluctance as a strategy in asymmetric warfare. Its defining feature is the employment of mass media to amplify indiscriminate, unconventional, and spectacular acts of violence, hoping thereby to undermine public support for those they oppose. The minutes are often written before the meeting, as any good secretary knows, but now they are being written neither by states nor terrorists, but by the employees of global news corporations.

If it aspires to disclose general truths about society, IR therefore needs to keep in mind that 'war' is a catch-all. Its causes, functions, and mores have varied across time and space. Perceptions of it have been shaped by forms of representation running from the Greek epic tradition of Homer through to the news bulletins of CNN. Social anthropologists were beginning to recognize this in the nineteenth century, when heads of state still thought waging war was their unconditional right, many lawyers regarded war as an act of God, and theologians – seemingly oblivious to the capabilities of new technologies of destruction – were returning to the medieval view that it could serve as an instrument of justice.

More recent work by ethno-historians has shown that war had radically different purposes in traditional political systems. Its function might be to acquire women or cattle among nomadic peoples with no fixed attachment to a specific territory. It has also shown that war may entirely fail in its regulatory function when fought between polities drawn from two different states-systems. Cultural difference may be so great that neither party understands the purpose for which the other is fighting or the conventions essential to that purpose. Aztecs were accustomed to fight in order to capture prestigious warriors for sacrifice. When they first encountered Spaniards they could not understand the insistence of the newcomers on killing, and found their resort to tactical withdrawal dishonourable. Radical destructive asymmetry, unprecedented levels of media manipulation, and Great Power acceptance of permanent killing zones in places thought strategically irrelevant now compound this historical variability.

The Causes of War

Enough has been said about the variable nature of war for it to be clear that any systematic explanation of its causes needs to be clear about exactly what sorts of conflict are to be examined. Historians have generally dodged the problem by avoiding generalization. They have been interested in the causes of specific wars. Why did war break out in Europe in 1914, or 1967, or 2003? But the historians have for the most part fallen in with the convention that proper wars are fought between well-established and substantial polities. Where one or more of the belligerents is not a state, it is assumed to be trying to gain control of an existing state (by civil war or rebellion) or to establish a new state (through secession or national liberation). Social scientists have generally shared this assumption, differing from the historians mainly by asking the more general question of why wars happen at all. They have characteristically offered explanations stressing human aggression, some distinctive characteristic of states, or the anarchic structure of the states-system: *Man, the State and War* in the title of Kenneth Waltz's celebrated study.

A war is not just a fight. Aggression is evident in hand-to-hand fighting or forms of combat requiring rapid response; perhaps less so in some other forms of modern warfare, such as the operation of drones from distant command and control centres. But to give it a prominent place in the causation of war is to concede too much to the influence of individuals, however powerful. Adolf Hitler, a favourite example of the leader bent on war, was the democratically elected leader of a nation where many – perhaps a majority – felt with some justification that they had been tricked by the November 1918 armistice and cheated in the subsequent peace negotiations. There was support for war, and the party and state apparatus that Hitler led – the regime – was as much responsible for German policy as he was himself. Like him they were responding to systemic pressures.

Social anthropologists were quick to recognize that the fundamentally co-operative and institutionalized – even ritualized – character of warfare made individual aggression of secondary importance in explaining war. In the first half of the twentieth century, when they were still characteristically preoccupied with small isolated communities, anthropologists generally preferred to claim that war, like language, was a cultural phenomenon, as different from aggression as is articulated speech from the trumpeting of an elephant. Alexander Lesser (1902–82), who studied under one of the founders of the discipline, Franz Boas (1858–1942), argued that it was inappropriate to speak of hostilities between simple kin groups as war. There might be fighting, surely, but war was something different and essentially political. With small and technologically pre-modern polities in mind he defined it as a struggle for scarce resources: for territory, women, and cattle. War, Lesser argued, arose out of the same circumstances that gave rise to the state, and was indeed conceivable only as a relationship between states. Long-distance trade and permanent settlement of land were the interlinked conditions for the independent development of state and war. Lesser concluded, optimistically, that war was not natural, but could be 'changed or eliminated, like any other political or cultural institution, by human planning or action'.

Another student of Boas, Margaret Mead (1901–78), advanced a different theory. Lesser thought that war was like language: cultural rather than natural, but not invented. Mead thought it more like the wheel: cultural *and* invented, but not everywhere. (There were no wheels in pre-Columbian America.) Mead attacked a particular variant of the security dilemma, which is the idea that one country's preparations to defend itself will be open to interpretation by its neighbour as preparations to attack, requiring counter-measures that initiate a vicious circle. To trust the assurances of the other is simply too great a risk. One version of the dilemma suggested that war was unavoidable in all but the most primitive cultures because the very political institutions needed to supervise long-distance trade and agriculture, while ensuring order within the community, could not but pose a threat to outsiders, so that war must be endemic in any states-system. Instead Mead argued that war was a functional response to specific circumstances and could in principle be got rid of once those circumstances no longer obtained. She found cultures, including cultures with high levels of expression of personal aggression (in the Arctic) that lacked the concept and institution of war, and others (in the Anderman Islands), too primitive to have developed war as a response to social complexity in the manner hypothesized by Lesser, yet which did engage in warfare. Mead concluded that, while inventions cannot be uninvented, some pass out of use because they are superseded by improved ways of performing the same function, opening the door to thoughts about peaceful conflict resolution and, in the words of Harvard psychologist William James (1842–1910), what might serve as 'the moral equivalent of war'.

Some modern sociobiologists have agreed with Mead about the inventedness of war but objected to her denial of its universality and selective function. War, spontaneously invented, spreads through contact until it is virtually universal. This cultural artefact creates the circumstances in which biological selection can operate an individual level in a culturally biased manner, since war brings prestige, wealth, wives, and offspring to those individuals who most excel in battle (and survive long enough to breed), while the mobility, disruption, and inter-breeding occasioned by war act to fragment kinship groups, making it impossible for warfare to act as an instrument of group selection.

Radically different in method and thinking from the CoW researchers, and from one another, both the anthropologists and the sociobiologists nevertheless belong in the same camp as the political scientists, because they locate the source of war in the characteristics of individual polities, rather than individual action or systemic pressure. Democratic peace theory is the strongest recent explanation of war – or rather its absence – as an outcome of characteristics of individual states, the units of the inter-state system. The observed regularity on which this theory rests is not that democracies are disinclined to fight undemocratic polities or are in any general way peaceable, but that they do not fight one another. The trouble is that the number of genuine democracies remained small until well into the twentieth century. Women did not gain equal voting rights with men in Britain until 1928, for example. Yet to limit the data set to the post-1945 period very considerably reduced the plausibility of the claim, since superpower rivalry and mutual deterrence meant that war among the client states of the USA or the USSR became almost impossible, while war between them – into which the superpowers might be drawn – was fraught with danger to the system as a whole. Worse, qualitative explanations of the observed infrequency of war between democracies have too often been vague about what was doing the work: liberalism, republicanism, democracy, or all three. This explanation teeters towards the systemic in its suggestion that particular *combinations* of regime type are likely to be conducive to war; but it stops short of a genuinely systemic explanation through its emphasis on a characteristic of the component units of the system rather than the system as a whole.

Some explanations occupy the border territory between unit-level and systemic neorealist theories. Though clearly rooted in the rational choice approach to politics, Stanford political scientist James Fearon has been at pains to identify himself with systemic neorealism. It is certainly true that the leading founder of neorealism, Kenneth Waltz, relied upon states acting rationally under anarchy to generate his theory of international politics, but his emphasis was rather more on the constraints imposed by anarchy than on the actively rational response of political actors to those constraints, while Fearon reverses the emphasis. His central concern is that states in conflict, knowing how uncertain and costly war can be, ought to be able 'to locate negotiated settlements that all would prefer to the gamble of war'. The question is why they cannot find a compromise that each would prefer even to a victory, since victory is never costless. The answer, which once again distinguishes his view from the highly abstract approach of Kenneth Waltz, is that lack of central authority (anarchy), expected benefit, precautionary anticipation, and rational miscalculation do not quite fit the bill. Instead he proposes that failure to reach a deal may arise from three problems. The first is that leaders may have secret information about relative military capabilities coupled with strong incentives not to disclose this information. This stems from something more than imperfect communication or misunderstanding; it suggests that there may be asymmetries of information built into anarchy. The second problem is that agreement may be impossible because it is apparent to both that one of the parties will have an incentive to renege on the agreement. Fearon calls this the 'commitment problem'. A third possibility is that states may fail to agree because they cannot separate the issue or issues at the heart of the conflict from other concerns or because what lies at the heart of the dispute simply is not open to compromise – Jerusalem, perhaps?

The fully systemic neorealist explanation of war is that the security dilemma makes co-operation a losing strategy for self-help units under anarchy. The system will gradually eliminate all states that do not provide for their own security by developing their capabilities or allying with one or other of the most powerful states. Within such a system relations between states will be perpetually tense. Suspicion and hostility will be endemic. Wars happen in such a system because states cannot risk not being in constant readiness. The only good news is that some distributions of capabilities across the system are more stable than others and that the security dilemma may therefore be less intransigent than used to be thought. Waltz himself was particularly attached to bipolarity and provided some powerful arguments in its favour. Others have favoured multipolarity. Still others think a unipolar or hegemonic system could be sustainable in the medium to long term so long as the hegemon behaves moderately. Historical research has suggested that multipolar balances have been less typical and hegemonic systems more common than once supposed.

Law of Armed Conflict and the Ethics of War

A pilot working with an allied force including US and British elements once quipped that if he was killed by his American colleagues he would have the consolation that they had almost certainly acted legally. The implication was that the Americans are almost obsessive about compliance with the law of armed conflict (international humanitarian law). This may be partly to avoid being portrayed as bullies and partly in order to hold on to the moral high ground while others are hauled before tribunals for their breaches of the laws of war and crimes against humanity. Indeed, it has been partly out of concern lest their own officers and leaders stand accused of war crimes that US administrations have held back from supporting the permanent International Criminal Court established in The Hague in 2002. The British, meanwhile, like to spread the idea that soldiers in a small volunteer army are a highly skilled and professional group of people who kill without anger and constitute a morally exemplary group within national society.

These caricatures have no more than a grain of truth. The contrast between the two is marginal: the Americans merely tending to legalism; the British tending towards professionalism, no more. Senior officer education in the USA is often superior. The US Marine Corps exudes moral superiority, not without justification. It is the smallest and most cohesive of the US armed forces, and its rigorous training programme instils Stoic values while insulating its members from society at large. The British are almost as law-obsessed as the Americans. Both have been accused on occasion of targeting errors resulting in civilian deaths and, more controversially, of initiating hostilities without clear legal authority, abusing prisoners, and conniving in the torture of prisoners. Each has its moral dark side: the strip joints and pawn shops that typically cluster near the gates of US bases; the damaged lives of those veterans who, on both sides of the Atlantic, account for a high proportion of the homeless and sick.

No wonder many scoff when they hear of courses in military academies and universities on the law or ethics of war. But such courses exist, and they are taken very seriously by commanders and politicians, determined that resort to force and the conduct of hostilities will not simply be politically prudent but also legally unimpeachable and morally defensible.

All this has been a long time in the making. In both Europe and the USA the development of modern international law can be traced to the second half of the nineteenth century. In so far as they were concerned with war, the lawyers initially set about regulating it but soon turned to the more ambitious task of eliminating or criminalizing it. International agreements before the First World War introduced new rules for the treatment of prisoners of war and banned weapons thought to cause needless suffering, such as the soft-pointed dum-dum bullets developed by the Indian Army in the 1890s, which fragmented after entering the body. As for war itself, it had long been accepted that European sovereigns had an absolute right to wage war against one another. Such argument as there was about the justice of war had been largely drained of its medieval moral or theological content. Over time, the absolute right had gradually normalized, with war thought by lawyers and statesmen to be allowable because it was consistent with the reproduction of the international system to which all states belonged. But by the end of the First World War, the sheer scale and destructiveness of the conflict had brought a change of mind.

When they drew up the 1919 Treaty of Versailles, the victors of the First World War included Article 227, which alleged that, by initiating hostilities in 1914 and violating the neutrality of Belgium and Luxembourg, the recently abdicated German Emperor, Wilhelm II, had committed 'a supreme offence against international morality and the sanctity of treaties'. The word crime appeared nowhere in this article, but the declared intention to bring him before a tribunal with judges empowered to determine what they might feel a suitable punishment strongly suggested that Wilhelm was being accused of a crime.

The Covenant of the League of Nations, which formed the first chapter of the Treaty of Versailles, was a further step towards the outlawing of war. The novel point was that war or the threat of war, whether or not it constituted a systemic risk, was now considered a matter for the League, that is to say the international community as a whole. Yet a succession of draft treaties, resolutions, and declarations asserting that war was a crime made little headway during the first postwar decade, whether at the League, in the Conference of American States, or in the US Senate. Even the Kellog–Briand Pact of 1928, which condemned war, fell short of any outright description of it as a crime or any specification of sanctions to be applied to those who perpetrated it. Not until 1945 would the United Nations, successor to the League, formally declare aggression to be a crime, effectively criminalizing any but a defensive war.

These persistent and ultimately successful attempts to criminalize aggression were given impetus by the First World War, but ought properly to be viewed as the outgrowth of a rising liberal conscience in the English-speaking and Protestant worlds that was complemented by a recovery of the medieval just war tradition within the Catholic Church. A fusion of the two was to dominate thought about the ethics of war by the turn of the twenty-first century.

The just war tradition goes back to St Augustine, but it was St Thomas Aquinas, almost a thousand years later, who laid the foundations of modern Catholic doctrine in this, as in so many other spheres. He and his Spanish Dominican successors wrote at a time – between 1200 and 1600 – when the monarchs of England, France, Spain, and several other European countries were steadily establishing sovereign authority over consolidated territories at the expense of Pope and Emperor. Towards the end of this period, orderly political communities were encountered in the Americas that had neither accepted nor – like the Turks – rejected the Christian gospel. This merely aggravated the emergent European challenge to papal and imperial authority. It confirmed the autonomy of international relations from any single faith community and exposed the anarchy of the system, now clearly seen to lack any supreme temporal authority capable of arbitrating between princes. In these circumstances a doctrine of how armed conflict between sovereigns of widely differing political communities could be contained within the moral and legal realm was sorely needed. This is what the later scholastic theologians provided and it has been revived in a modified form in recent decades.

Reduced to its bare bones, the early modern just war doctrine runs like this. Justified resort to war requires a formal declaration of hostilities – all other remedies having been exhausted – by a proper authority with a reasonable prospect of victory, moved by right intention to make good an injury or wrong of sufficient importance to outweigh the unavoidable evils that will result from the conduct of hostilities. Once engaged in warfare, combatants are enjoined not to attack non-combatants and to use no more force than is needed to achieve their military objectives.

Some of the contemporary debates within the tradition leap from the page. Where is legitimate authority to be found in a world where many states have long since lost control of large tracts of their territory and armed groups batten on populations without any clear political programme or aspiration to statehood? Where is legitimate authority to be found in a world where permanent alliances or regional unions such as NATO or the European Union have begun to acquire a measure of autonomy, even from their most powerful members, yet have only limited democratic accountability? What price legitimate authority when uncertainty about the authority of the UN Security Council is aggravated by the pretensions of the United States to a quasi-imperial regulatory role?

How are we to regard collateral damage? Is it justified as a means to the successful achievement of a military objective, or must it be the unintended outcome of an attack upon a legitimate target. In the doctrine of double effect, Catholic theologians have ingeniously excused the harm done to civilians in war, even when it was foreseeable, provided the primary intention was to restore peace by imposing justice.

Do precision-guided munitions make the dilemmas of unintended harm easier or more difficult to cope with? Mistakes, such as the destruction of the Chinese embassy in Belgrade in 1999, become less credible. Assassination becomes much easier: it was attempted against Saddam Hussein at the very start of the Third Gulf War in 2003 and accomplished against Osama Bin Laden in 2011. It has since become routine in US operations in Afghanistan and Pakistan, but is it morally acceptable? What of military contractors engaging in logistical and support activities near the battlefield? Are they non-combatants? What of reservoirs, telecommunications equipment, transport infrastructure, all of which serve civilian as well as military purposes? Does the distinction on which discrimination relies any longer make sense? What of nuclear deterrence? How can the use of weapons of mass destruction ever avoid harm to non-combatants? How may the unintended harm it would inflict on non-combatants ever be thought proportionate either to the wrong that gave rise to a conflict or to any military objective? More subtly, can it be right to threaten to do wrong if by so doing one minimizes the chance of ever having to carry out the threat? Can military personnel be trained and equipped to carry out nuclear attacks, their missiles targeted on enemy cities, without being corrupted by the intention to do what could never justifiably be done?

The undoubted value and popularity of the just war tradition lie in the framework it provides for people of any faith or none to debate a wide range of moral questions arising from armed conflict. It is sufficiently flexible to accommodate discussion of the conclusion of wars, which some have claimed requires a supplement, a *jus post bellum*, or law after war, to add to the *jus ad bellum* (justifying resort to war), and *jus in bello* (governing the conduct of hostilities). But the *jus post bellum* has been there from the start in right intention, which must always include achievement of a just peace.

Yet three grave problems afflict the tradition. The first is its profoundly state-centric character. Aquinas was concerned to draw a line between public warfare, between sovereigns, and private wars. This was a move in the late-medieval political game of sorting out just which of the innumerable titles held by members of the European nobility conferred sovereignty. This is what the proper authority condition was all about. To try to extend the tradition to cover non-state actors is therefore a profound mistake. Not only was the doctrine not intended to cover them, it was specifically designed to exclude them.

The second problem is that the tradition is inconsistent with international law. The glaring inconsistency between these two movements was evident at least from the 1930s. By that time revival of the ideas of sixteenth-century Spanish Dominican Francisco de Vitoria was in full swing, led by leading US lawyer James Brown Scott (1866–1943). Liberals and lawyers were out to eliminate war; the just war tradition, by contrast, had always been concerned to justify and regulate it. In spite of this, many people confuse the two because international lawyers appropriated the tradition as part of a retrospective history of their upstart branch of legal studies, and even embraced some elements of it, such as the immunity of non-combatants. But on the crucial question of just cause, international law had eliminated all grounds except defence against aggression by the middle of the twentieth century. Ruling out of court all aspects of a dispute, aside from who shot first, is tough on irascible states with a case they just might win if they could only get it to court. Many Argentines would agree, arguing that the strength of their legal claim to islands in the South Atlantic governed by Britain was sufficient to justify resort to force in 1982 after seventeen years of talks had failed to achieve a mutually satisfactory solution. Others would feel that pre-emptive and preventive military action is justified only in the face of imminent threat of attack, which was certainly not the Argentine case in 1982.

The practical value and moral justification of a pre-emptive strike when the enemy's intended aggression is blatant can seem overwhelming. Moral justification for a preventive attack on a country seemingly intent on developing weapons of mass destruction (WMDs) is less clear. This was the pretext for the 2003 Allied invasion of Iraq, which so signally failed to find the suspected WMDs. The invasions of Iraq in 2003 and the Falkland Islands in 1982 suggest that to replace currently restrictive law with pure Catholic doctrine would be to visit innumerable wars upon the world. The only requirement would be that a state felt it had a good case. The tradition does not offer clear rules or law, but a set of considerations. This flexibility is as much a source of weakness as of strength.

Indeed, the concern of Phillip Gray, a US scholar whose book on the just war is grounded in a profound understanding of Catholic theology, is that without its underlying theological assumptions the tradition loses coherence. This is the third problem afflicting the just war tradition. Carl Schmitt (1888–1985), a German jurist writing soon after the Second World War, agreed. 'If today some formulas of the doctrine of just war, rooted in the institutional order of the medieval *respublica Christiana*, are utilized in modern and global formulas,' he wrote, 'this does not signify a return to, but rather a fundamental transformation of concepts of enemy, war, concrete order, and justice presupposed in medieval doctrine'. If war ceases to be regarded as an instrument of divine providence and proper authority becomes detached from Catholic understandings of political community, then the tradition very soon becomes a mere checklist capable of achieving precisely opposite results for hawks (aggressors) and doves (peace-seekers). For non-Christians, it is almost certainly safer to resist the undoubted intellectual attractions of Catholic doctrine and stick with law.

The Transformative Effects of War

While it was essentially a struggle between states, total warfare over the past two hundred years has shaped the armed forces of the major powers, requiring their professionalization, their command of rapidly changing technologies, their seclusion in barracks and camps, and their management of multitudes of conscripts in times of war. It has also required the mobilization of whole nations, riding roughshod over custom and property rights. The first of these processes is best thought of as a transformation in military ethics; the second, as a painful process of successive dislocations and intensifications of political loyalties, above all sentiments of patriotism and nationalism.

Military ethics is not the same thing as the ethics of war. The latter is a direct concern of states and therefore an integral aspect of international relations. Military ethics is much more a concern of individuals serving in armed forces, and the units in which they serve, though states bear considerable and ultimate responsibility for it, and for the ways in which it influences combat, through their recruitment and training of combatants, their general treatment of the armed forces, and their responses to the conduct of their troops. The two converge in that division of just war thinking concerned with the conduct of hostilities, the *jus in bello*.

The reason for considering this aspect of warfare from the perspective of those who served in armed forces is that their typical range of experience has become steadily more distinct from that of most statesmen and politicians. Military ethics grows out of the *practice* and experience of warfare rather than from the debates of theologians or lawyers, and it has often sat uncomfortably beside just war doctrine and international humanitarian law. Resistance to just war thinking has been especially notable since asymmetric and irregular forms of warfare replaced the Cold War stand-off. Perhaps it is because they have felt live metal whistling past that the some of the most resilient exponents of a broad view of military ethics have been former officers teaching in military establishments. It is worth recalling that Carl von Clausewitz (1780–1831), the paramount philosopher of modern war, had seen active service in the armies of Prussia and Russia, including the battles of Jena (1806) and Borodino (1812), before his appointment in 1818 as director of the Prussian military academy.

The military academies and staff colleges have their share of just war theorists, but they are also home to a much broader tradition, evident in recent anthologies designed as course texts, as well as in monographs by those who teach there, some of them veterans, others not. Together, these works have emphasized the relevance to military life of a variety of traditions of moral philosophy including Aristotelian virtue ethics and Stoicism. Harking back to the eighteenth-century Scottish Enlightenment thinker Adam Ferguson, and beyond, to Machiavelli, they also recognized the distinctive importance of the military as a repository of much that is best and worst in society, finding military virtues among the scum of the earth. In its commentary on contemporary society Thomas Ricks' *Making the Corp* stands in a long and distinguished tradition. Ricks traced a group of fifty recruits through initial Marine training and dwelt on the gulf between the qualities that training and subsequent service aspired to develop and the demoralized condition of those parts of American society from which the volunteers were drawn. There is much more to this than the deep conservatism of Robert Heinlein's *Starship Troopers*, in which political rights are reserved exclusively to veterans, or the cynical and exclusionary arrogance of Jack Nicholson's Marine colonel in *A Few Good Men* (1992).

In addition to experience and observation, those teaching in the military academies and war colleges have been able to draw on customary treatments of war in films, memoirs, novels, and plays, which have provided a continuous strand of European literature since the chronicles of the late medieval period. Chivalric codes, customary laws of war, and plain drill have had at least as much purchase on behaviour in combat as *jus in bello* or humanitarian law. This is another of the many areas in which it is helpful to distinguish between International Politics, with its state-centric or realist worldview, and the wider and more inclusive vision of International Relations. When it turns its attention to ethics, International Politics is not unnaturally concerned with the deliberations of sovereigns, but IR sweeps a wider horizon. It is clear that soldiers have been more prone to live truly global lives than most members of the populations from which they have been drawn, whether in mixed imperial forces, as mercenaries, or in national expeditionary forces. The discontinuity, incompleteness, and contradictions of the just war in recent times have created space for a rival tradition of military ethics to become visible once again.

Examples abound of war stories with moral relevance but little just war resonance. Some characterize the soldier as witness, pilgrim, or even Christ. Others represent war as an excess or fragmentation of reason. Stephen Crane's anti-hero in *The Red Badge of Courage* remains a witness to battle, constantly rehearsing heroics in his mind even when his body is in the thick of it. For some, such as Guy Crouchback, the central character in Evelyn Waugh's Second World War trilogy *Sword of Honour*, and

John Buchan's Richard Hannay, war constitutes a pilgrimage. This is pressed home by Buchan in *Mr Standfast* (1919) through repeated reference to John Bunyan's 1678 *The Pilgrim's Progress*. Gillo Pontecorvo, secular north-Italian Jew and former Marxist partisan, took things a stage further by drawing a close analogy between Christ and his anti-hero, the erstwhile petty criminal Ali La Pointe, in *The Battle of Algiers*, his compelling 1966 film about the urban terrorist stage of the Algerian struggle for independence. For Joseph Heller the Second World War becomes emblematic of the extreme paradoxes of liberal rationality. It is a world where market forces can leave the officers of a USAAF squadron with no option but to bomb their own base. For Kurt Vonnegut the same war can be represented only through a narrative of dislocation in which Billy Pilgrim (note the name), a draftee chaplain's assistant who never encounters combat (or a chaplain), is shaken loose from his moorings in time and space by witnessing the Allied destruction of Dresden: a life in disarray, its formation utterly disordered.

War is too important and too intrusive to be left to politicians or soldiers. It is transformative of individuals, including non-combatants, and of whole societies. Its prevalence, variety, and endless openness to interpretation place it alongside peacetime economic pursuits as a leading element in international relations. Many of the social changes wrought by the world wars of the twentieth century were felt most strongly within nations rather than in their relations with one another. Examples include the mobilization of women, many of whom subsequently refused to return to pre-war domesticity. But the most profound effect was to enhance national consciousness and, in many countries, to foster organized nationalist parties.

This impact on international social relations was evident in three ways. The first of these was the displacement of large numbers of people fleeing from hostilities or persecution. One direct consequence of this was the creation of the State of Israel in May 1948. But the war also left substantial displaced minorities permanently stranded far from home without any form of collective political expression or representation. Perhaps as many as a million people of Polish descent live in Argentina today. This migration began before the world wars, but it was especially after 1945 that Argentina provided a haven for displaced Poles, for whom return to communist Poland would have been fatal.

A second global consequence of the world wars was a weakening of deference towards Europeans, hastening the end of empire in Africa, Asia, and the Caribbean. Troops from European dependencies reacted in various ways to service in the world wars. For some it brought experience of command and responsibility that groomed them for leadership on their return home. For others it was the prelude to postwar migration to European cities. Still others responded to the inadequacies of their European masters in the face of war, whether at tactical or strategic level, by joining the rank and file of postwar nationalist movements.

Respect for Europeans and Americans could not survive the sight of their humiliation, in retreat or as prisoners. Worst of all, for their effect on prestige, were the extraordinary speed and extent of Japanese victories in a little over two months, starting with the attack on Pearl Harbor in December 1941 and ending with British defeat in Singapore in February 1942. The attack on Pearl Harbor was designed to eliminate the near certainty of US intervention to obstruct the imminent Japanese southward drive to seize Dutch oilfields in Indonesia. It achieved its purpose by sinking four US battleships and damaging four more, along with many other vessels and 188 aircraft. With this objective accomplished, the principal remaining obstacle to Japanese capture of the oilfields was the British fortress of Singapore. There, the city's defences had been reinforced at great expense in the 1930s. Supported by modern aircraft and a naval squadron, the British colony was thought impregnable to attack from the sea. But by February 1942 the Japanese had eliminated the Royal Air Force, sunk the two British capital ships, and pushed British and Australian land forces back on Singapore in disarray. A land attack on the city had never been anticipated. With their artillery pointed the wrong way, their water supply vulnerable, and their 100,000 troops hopelessly penned in, the British had no choice but to surrender. The rest of the world witnessed these humiliations. Seemingly powerful states had proved unable to protect their dependent territories and allies. People drew their own conclusions; reimposition of empire after the end of the war would be neither easy nor permanent in the face of nationalist opposition.

A third effect of the war on international relations and domestic politics alike was that promises had to be made to domestic constituencies, dependent peoples, allies, and neutrals alike. These great wars were allegedly being fought by democracies against autocracy between 1914 and 1918 and totalitarianism in the 1940s. But for this claim to be plausible, promises had to be made. At home this meant that there must be no return to the high unemployment of the interwar years. In the wider world it meant that some means must be found to ensure collective security by averting future wars. The League of Nations aspired to do this after the First World War, but failed. After 1945 a second global objective emerged, which was to prevent global economic disruption. The result was the United Nations system and the Bretton Woods institutions. But individual allied nations had also to be rewarded. Brazil, the most active of the Latin American states in the Second World War, looked to the USA to place Latin American economic development on a par with European recovery, to which the USA had committed $13 billion in the 1948 Marshall Plan. The 1961 Alliance for Progress was the more modest and ideologically charged result. The British had been obliged to make concessions to India, the cornerstone of its empire, during the First World War. The Second World War made independence inevitable, and the final transfer of power took place in 1947. Other European dependencies soon followed. More broadly, the values expressed by the victorious powers and enunciated in the Universal Declaration of Human Rights, approved by the UN General Assembly in 1948, could and would be deployed by the colonized against their masters in dozens of independence struggles.

War in the twentieth century did not simply redraw political maps and adjust the balance of power between states. It transformed millions of lives, in many cases forcing individuals, as conscripts or refugees, to move from places where they might otherwise have spent their whole lives, to compare one state with another, and to reconsider political loyalties. It also wrought profound changes in the profession of arms, affecting the lives of those on whom the burden of international relations falls most heavily when international politics and diplomacy fail.

5
Making sense of international relations

The standard account of the origins of IR runs something like this. In the immediate aftermath of the First World War, governments and philanthropists in the United States and Britain, determined that there should never be any repetition of war on the unprecedented scale that they had just witnessed, set up institutions designed to avert future wars. These institutions reflected prevailing opinion on the origins of the war. Lack of democratic openness in foreign policy-making, imperial rivalries, arms racing, militarism, and the formation of opposing alliance systems had been among the leading causes. Further development of international law, the promotion of collective security through the League of Nations, a requirement that the vanquished nations pay reparations to the victors, constraints on their future acquisition of armaments, and the dismantling of their colonial empires were among the remedies proposed, consistent with the manifesto that had been set out by US President Woodrow Wilson – his 'Fourteen Points'.

For the history of IR the most important of the supposed causes of the war is undoubtedly lack of democratic control over foreign policy-making. Here it was felt that greater public awareness and open discussion between political, business, and academic elites would help ensure that decisions were taken in the national interest, and not for the benefit of some narrow section of the population, be they aristocrats or financiers. Populist tracts and Hobson's *Imperialism* (1902), with its critique of the manipulation of foreign policy by big business, had evidently been widely read. It was in this spirit that university departments and research institutes were set up immediately after the war. The Council on Foreign Relations in the United States and the Royal Institute of International Affairs in London, better known as Chatham House, from the building that still houses it today, were originally intended to be a single transatlantic institution. Both existed to keep open channels of information and influence between government and elites. University departments were established and professorial chairs endowed. The Montagu Burton Chair at the LSE – the London School of Economics and Political Science, to give it its full title – was established in 1924. But the first chair in Britain was, curiously, the result of a 1919 bequest to the University of Wales by Lord David Davies (1880–1944), heir to a substantial coal fortune. This resulted in the unlikely creation in a tiny and remote seaside town of what remains one of the leading departments in the UK. In the United States the first graduate programme was set up in 1928 at the University of Chicago. Other pioneering schools included the School of Advanced International Studies at Johns Hopkins University in Baltimore; the Fletcher School at Tufts; and the School of International and Public Affairs at Columbia University, in New York City.

Often those appointed to these new university positions were expected not only to teach and conduct research but also actively to promote good relations between states. The Wilson chair, endowed by Davies and named for President Woodrow Wilson, required that the professor should spend some of his time travelling and promoting peace in order to accomplish this. There was to be a two-way dialogue between academic and practitioner, truth and power. Davies himself had served in the First World War. A close associate of wartime prime minister David Lloyd

George, he represented a Welsh constituency from 1906–29 in the House of Commons and, in 1930, produced a plan to bring an end to war by creating a multinational force able to deter aggression.

These academic developments were flanked by widespread support for peace movements, public interest in the fledgling League of Nations, and an upsurge in faith in the ability of international organizations and international law to constrain states. It was at this point that functionalist theory crystallized. This was the view that public loyalty to militaristic states could be reduced to the extent that people saw that their welfare depended on international organizations, each with a specific 'function', like control of epidemic diseases or the trade in narcotic drugs. David Mitrany, who had been educated at the LSE just before the outbreak of the First World War, became a member of the Fabian Society, a group of socialists who believed in gradual reform and opposed revolution. Until 1931 he also served on the British Labour Party's Advisory Committee on International Questions, chaired by Leonard Woolf, another pioneer of functionalism. Influenced by Woolf's 1916 *International Government*, Mitrany argued that the ever more complex character of the modern world meant that populations were becoming more and more dependent on services that could only be provided through international co-operation. International provision would start with the integration of relatively uncontroversial services, often referred to as 'low' politics, and then gradually move into more contentious areas of 'high' politics. By placing the headquarters of each new international organization in a different city, power could be decentralized.

Law figured more prominently than organization in American thought during the 1920s. This was partly because the US Congress blocked membership of the League of Nations, leading to a temporary disengagement of the USA from the conduct of grand strategy. A second factor was that powerful elements in the US Republican Party had already, years before the World War, pinned their hopes for improved international relations on the deliberate crafting and codification of international law, both hemispheric and universal, rather than functional co-operation. This was not unnatural given the very large size of the USA and its lack of neighbours relative to the states of Europe. It took the form of a process, captured in the slogan 'Peace through Law' and soon to be denigrated as idealistic or utopian, that culminated in the 1928 General Treaty for the Renunciation of War. The treaty is more often referred to as the Kellog–Briand Pact, so named for its chief architects, US Secretary of State Frank B. Kellog and French Foreign Minister Aristide Briand.

This standard account has been modified in no less than five ways by recent scholarship. First, some of the arguments and initiatives once thought wholly reactive to the First World War and characteristic of the 1920s have been found to antedate the war. IR was in some law schools in embryo form before 1914, in the influential London School of Economics, and in public debate. Second, the disciplinary history sketched in E.H. Carr's powerful 1939 introduction to IR, *The Twenty Years' Crisis*, which traces a sharp move from 1920s utopianism to 1930s realism, has been exposed as a gross oversimplification, constructed retrospectively for polemical purposes. It exaggerated the extent of the transformation, marginalized many competing currents of thought, and over-dramatized international thought of the period as a kind of duel or 'great debate'. Third, the advocates of peace-through-law and functionalism were less idealistic and theoretical than Carr claimed. The British Labour Party Advisory Committee, on which functionalists Mitrany and Woolf served, looks more realist than idealist when closely scrutinized. International law served, for the USA, as an effective form of soft power or low politics in the period during which the country had not yet attained Great Power, let alone superpower status. Fourth, realism was less uniform and secular than Carr suggested.

In the USA there was a strong following for the Christian realism of American theologian Reinhold Niebuhr, whose work Carr admired. In Cambridge, Methodist lay preacher and historian Herbert Butterfield chaired the British Committee on the Theory of International Relations, and his brand of explicitly religious thought about international relations held its place in public debate into the 1960s. A final consideration is that the old foundational myth of IR concentrates too much on the period before 1939. On the one hand, traces of IR can be detected before 1914, but on the other it is incontestable that IR was marginal in US and British academic life until *after* the Second World War.

One kind of misleading retrospective history can be laid squarely at the door of Carr, the British diplomat turned scholar–journalist. A second – while present in Carr's work – has more diffuse origins. This is the recruitment of past thinkers, reaching back to antiquity, into rival teams to compete in some kind of intellectual World Series or Olympic Games. The realists get to choose Hegel, Hobbes, Machiavelli, and Thucydides. The liberals take Jeremy Bentham, Immanuel Kant, the Abbé Saint-Pierre, Adam Smith, and Woodrow Wilson. Some commentators have preferred three traditions. Martin Wight went for the alliterative trio of Realist, Rationalist, and Revolutionist, captained by Hobbes, Grotius, and Kant respectively. There's a good deal of quibbling about where Jean-Jacques Rousseau, Edmund Burke, and Karl Marx belong. All of these authors are worth reading. Some have profound things to say about international relations. But what is objectionable about IR's co-opting of past thought is its magpie method, picking out bright fragments with little regard for the political context in which they were written, the general arguments in which they were originally embedded, or the contemporary debates to which their authors were contributing. Recent scholarship has gone far to apologise for the promiscuity of the founding generation, repairing the breach with more scholarly history of political thought, but this remains just one more area of history where IR must tread very carefully to avoid blunders and where seeming lessons from history have to be heavily discounted to allow for the radical differences between present and past.

Academic IR developed in the midst of a group of social sciences, including philosophy, economics, sociology, anthropology, and political science, in which a great many terms had already acquired established and often complex meanings. The central opposition in IR has been cast as one between realists and liberals, but the words 'utopian' and 'idealist' have sometimes been used as substitutes for 'liberal'. Yet to philosophers 'idealist' brings to mind the German idealists of the early nineteenth century, including Hegel, who has just been mentioned as a proto-realist in IR. 'Rationalist', which Wight appropriated for one of his three traditions, is conventionally used to describe philosophers, such as Descartes, Leibniz, and Spinoza, who believe that our knowledge of the world does not derive solely from sense experience. This is not how Wight used the word. Before long we shall return to that treacherous term 'positivist'. Even 'liberal' is tricky because it denotes a broad intellectual tradition but is also part of the name of many political parties, and has quite different resonances in the United States and Britain. IR scholars have been inclined to latch on to words suited to their purposes but often apply them in ways quite inconsistent with their established meanings.

IR Since 1945

The outstanding features of the history of IR since the Second World War have been the rapid increase in its popularity, a spawning of sub-fields, the claims of successive varieties of realism to constitute an orthodoxy, and a general preoccupation with method.

There are several reasons for this increase in popularity, including increased opportunities to play a practical part in international affairs through employment in global corporations, IGOs, and INGOs. The profusion of sub-fields and study groups partly reflects this growth in scale. With so many more IR departments in universities, the annual congress of the International Studies Association, the US-based multinational professional body of IR scholars, has become a massive event with several thousand delegates.

It was inevitable that here, as in any other academic field, specialization would develop. There are now more than twenty thematic sections in the ISA, including diplomatic studies, feminist theory, and international law. The development of International Political Economy is a special case of sub-field development, in that it is not simply identified by its subject matter but also a partial solution to two characteristic problems of IR. These are the questions of how IR should interface with related disciplines in general and with International Politics in particular. Following from this, it bears on the third feature of post-1945 IR, which is the claim of realism to pre-eminence or orthodoxy. With some exceptions, realists have tended to marginalize international economic relations. Their critics have been more attentive to the global economy.

In the mid-1970s, as the field of economics became ever more technical and the Bretton Woods system and North–South relations reached crisis point, a number of economists felt that IR was losing touch with reality, taught exclusively by historians, political scientists, lawyers, and retired diplomats who did not fully grasp the enormity of the crisis facing the postwar settlement. Pioneer publications by men and women who could remember the Second World War and the world depression that preceded it made it possible to introduce university courses that were neither world economic history nor the history of economic thought, still less international economics, but had elements of all three. Soon afterwards the first textbooks followed. Their carefully phrased titles, and those of some of the pioneering works of the 1970s, reveal changing methodological and disciplinary orientations as well as the preferences of authors and publishers. *Power and Money: The Economics of International Politics and the Politics of International Economics* (1970), suggestive of interaction between quite distinct disciplines, was followed by *Power and Wealth: The Political Economy of International Power* (1973). Within a few years the compromise suggested by the second of these titles had been abandoned or appropriated, as Political Science and IR claimed a new and popular sub-field with the *The Politics of International Economic Relations* (1978) and *The Political Economy of International Relations* (1987).

The invention of IPE solved one manifestation of what might be called the Dutch problem. How can IR do justice to every discipline that bears on its concerns? The answer, of course, is that it cannot, and that the formation of buffer fields such as IPE is a practicable solution only where the subject matter is of pressing importance and the language and techniques of the authoritative discipline forbidding. A second solution has been to attempt the laudable multidisciplinarity of postwar Dutch political science within confined institutions, where the intellectual compromises imposed by the requirements of professional training can be shielded from general view. The model here is the seminary rather than the university, with military staff colleges and diplomatic academies the leading exemplars in IR.

The Dutch Problem

Late in life, Jacques Thomassen, a distinguished scholar from the Netherlands, reminisced about the origin of what he called 'political science' in the Netherlands following the end of the Second World War. The founders were keen to differentiate themselves from their contemporaries in the USA, who were starting to model political science on economics or the natural sciences and were very insistent on its disciplinary autonomy. He outlined what I have referred to as the Dutch problem:

> 'The new program was not narrowly focused on political sci-
> ence alone. In its curriculum political science proper was only one
> of the major fields in addition to economics, modern history, law
> and sociology. However the professors responsible for these fields
> had no intention to make any concessions to students in the new
> program, and demanded full knowledge of their respective dis-
> ciplines. As a consequence, the cumulative demands on students
> were impossible. Less than ten percent of the first student cohorts
> reached the finish and received the degree ... The few who did so
> had studied more than nine years on average.'

Within the universities, the Dutch problem has characteristically
been solved by establishing a dominant position for International
Politics within IR. One interesting example of how this tactic
differs from that of more specialized academies is the broad
approach to ethics adopted in US military academies, contrasted
with a preference for a state-centric reading of the just war
tradition in universities. But the International Politics strategy has
been widespread, strengthened, if anything, by the oppositional
posture of many of its critics, who like to be seen battling against
a conservative mainstream, and have therefore colluded in
fostering the myth of realist dominance of IR. This loads the dice
in favour of IP, because emphasis on the centrality of the state
and subordination of economic affairs are regarded as consistent
features of political realism, often conjoined with emphasis on
power, national interest, the intransigence of conflict, the difficulty
of co-operation, and a fatalistic pessimism.

Widespread 1970s insistence on the importance of economics
appeared to challenge the pretentions of realism. A Marxist strand
within IPE really did so by contesting the categories of the
political and the economic, preferring to draw the line between
the material base and the superstructural or institutional forms
of society. But liberal varieties of IPE, which became dominant
as the 1980s progressed, emphasized interaction *between* grand
abstractions – the economic and the political – in order to shield

the autonomy and primacy of the political from erosion by any more inclusive and holistic vision of world society. Once again the titles of some of the pioneering books tell the story: *Power and Money, Power and Wealth, The Economics of International Politics,* and *The Politics of International Economics.* Each in its different way bore witness to the struggle to affirm disciplinary boundaries and state-sovereignty while dealing with events that transgressed both. International Political Economy was from the very beginning a methodological and ideological battlefield, and the brilliance of the name lies in the way it wobbles unsteadily between its three component terms, never quite settling.

By the late 1970s IPE was settling down as a form of economics for non-economists, performing two ideological functions. The first was to reproduce the standard IR divisions between politics and economics and between realist and liberal; its generally acknowledged status as sub-field gently but firmly privileged the first of each of these two pairs. Second, it provided a stage for the final appearance of Marxist thought within the US academy. Then, as the country reeled from defeat in Vietnam, the shaming of President Nixon, and unprecedented oil prices, breathing space was required while a convincing reassertion of IP was mounted, able to claim the scientific high ground and make use of economics while firmly relegating it to a supporting role. This was the *Theory of International Politics.* In this very influential book, Kenneth Waltz drew an analogy between global oligopolistic competition and the balance of power. But he was very firm in maintaining the separation of the two realms: global markets and the anarchic inter-state system. To suggest that outcomes in the latter arose from economic causes was reductionist, he maintained, like trying to explain genetics by resorting to small particle physics. Since states ultimately set the terms on which firms operated, the primacy of the political was maintained.

So what IPE did for the academy was to maintain a vital pillar of liberal thought – the analytical separation of economics and politics – by framing the 1970s crisis as one of interaction between the two. It provided a safe space in which to examine these interactions without compromising the integrity of International Politics, which dealt with the relatively autonomous play of state power. Finally, it allowed the postwar narrative of the discipline to form around the issue of co-operation rather than any more profound transformation of the global economy. The way this came about was that some aspects of globalization, such as the emergence of TNCs and experiments with regional integration, were deemed to be clearly economic. As such they were dealt with by IPE. Meanwhile, within International Politics, more or less the same empirical material fuelled abstract debates between neorealists and neo-liberals about global legal and institutional regimes, the possibilities of sustained co-operation, and balancing. This division of debate about globalization into IPE and IP strands made plausible a disciplinary IR narrative in which realism weathered a series of challenges to its dominance. It withstood each successive shock, replicating itself, confusingly, into structural, defensive, offensive, and neoclassical variants, and coming out stronger every time. Sometimes, the challenge has stemmed from the surprising ability of states to continue to co-operate even when the global economy slips into recession; at other times, apparent shifts in the distribution of global power have prompted theoretical revision, most of all following the collapse of the Soviet Union. Frequently, the impetus for change has been internal, as the field repeatedly renewed its vow to be more scientific.

The supposed dominance of realism has depended on the insulation of international economic relations, the privileging of IP within IR, astute response to events, and, finally, the ability to preserve the realist brand while its content changed almost beyond recognition. Methodological inconsistency has been the key to the longevity of realism. Starting as little more than armchair speculation informed by the extensive but unsystematic knowledge of practitioners, modern political realism pulled off the rather impressive trick of forcing liberalism on to the back foot. This was achieved in part by the creation of a largely imaginary lineage stretching back through Hobbes and Machiavelli to Thucydides, while renaming liberalism as idealism or utopianism and painting it as a naive response to the Great War of 1914–18. This rhetorical manoeuvre concealed the patent truth that liberalism had been engaged in a continuous and prominent debate about commerce, war, and their interaction since the eighteenth century. This tradition had far more substance than any realist tradition and its pure or 'classical' form had, by the early twentieth century, engendered powerful Marxist and compensatory or welfarist variants.

The masterstroke of neorealism at the end of the 1970s was its appropriation of the high status of the natural sciences. But initially, in the 1960s, it was idealists rather than realists who made a grab for science, adopting the inductive method by which empirical observation of law-like regularities was regarded as the only sure basis for the construction of theories. The objective of the inductivist social scientists who founded the Correlates of War project was to eliminate war. Disparaging the armchair methods of the classical realists, they were not prepared to accept that war was simply an ineradicable feature of international relations or that knowing what caused war might not enable political leaders to avoid it, even if they wanted to. The only way they differed from liberals, committed to international organization, education, and law, was in their commitment to positivism as a philosophical position and a practical methodology.

In this fixation on the application of the supposed methods of the natural sciences to society, the 1960s positivists were the heirs to French positivism of the early nineteenth century. As formulated by Henri de Saint-Simon and Auguste Comte, positivism supposed the senses to be the sole source of reliable knowledge, eschewing all unobservable entities: liberal faith in a secularized providence just as much as Christian belief in spirit and deity. The Péreire brothers, Émile and Isaac, built the first railway in France in 1835 and went on to create a vast business empire comprising urban utilities, insurance, and shipping. But their global influence rested primarily in the novel use of banking to foster economic development and industrialization – today's investment banking – and their fusing of this with explicit commitment to technological progress and dismissal of the unobservable.

Positivists also made a strong showing in legal thinking, insisting that the only true law was the command of a sovereign backed by sanctions and scorning Christian belief in natural law, supposedly latent in God's creation and waiting to be discovered. Later in the century positivism took root in several Latin American republics and began somewhat ironically to assume the form of a church, with congregations of the faithful meeting in secular temples as far afield as London and Porto Alegre, Brazil. What the 1960s IR inductivists inherited from this rich tradition was their faith in the ease with which observations about the world could be reported. This rested on a naive belief in the correspondence between words and the things they described, and between claims about the world and the world itself (propositions and facts). In addition they shared, with earlier positivists, a belief in the possibility of social engineering. This marked them off from the more individualist kind of liberal because it required state intervention.

Hard on the heels of the 1960s inductivists came a second wave of self-consciously scientific IR scholars, now concerned rather more with structure and interaction than with the law-like regularities and regression analyses of the CoW project. Here too there were elements of positivism. The security dilemma, it may be recalled, arose when one state's defensive moves provoked the military preparations of its neighbour until both were embroiled in a confrontation desired by neither. Urgency was imparted to the work of IR scholars in the 1960s by a nuclear confrontation between the superpowers that could be seen as a particularly intransigent example of this. Herbert Butterfield, a British realist of the old school, saw this as a predicament from which humanity could escape only through the grace of God. The younger generation in the USA, drawing on game theory – a branch of mathematics – at first thought it inescapable. Later Robert Axelrod used ever more inexpensive computing power to run strategies by which, over an extended sequence of plays, co-operation could evolve without divine intervention. The security dilemma could, in principle, be overcome.

The game of 'prisoners' dilemma' models the security dilemma. Two partners in crime are arrested by the authorities and each is placed in solitary confinement. Communication is impossible. The police lack sufficient evidence to secure a conviction, but in this imagined country a prisoner can be detained for up to six months without formal charges being brought. Each is offered a deal. Confess, give evidence against your partner and you will go free, while he serves a two-year sentence. It seems too good to be true until the prosecutor admits that if the testimony is not required, because the other prisoner has confessed, then both will serve the reduced term of eighteen months. If both remain silent, the joint term of imprisonment is twelve months. If both confess, the joint term is thirty-six months. If only one prisoner confesses, he goes free and his partner serves two years, making a joint sentence of twenty-four months. It is obvious to both men that the best joint outcome available to them is to stay silent. After all, twelve is half of twenty-four and a third of thirty-six. But each is aware that his partner may be tempted by the prospect of immediate freedom, and although you might say that two years in jail is not the worst *joint* outcome of the game, it is clearly the worst outcome for whoever serves all twenty-four months.

The only way to be sure of avoiding that fate is to confess, even though this course of action risks an eighteen-month sentence. Since each prisoner sees that if he can grasp this then it won't be long before his partner does, they both confess. Each avoids the worst *individual* outcome, but they end up with the worst possible *joint* outcome, a full three years of servitude between them. The puzzle is how, without communication, the two prisoners can co-operate to get at the best joint outcome while each avoids the worst individual outcome that will assuredly await him should his partner defect. The analogy with the security dilemma works like this: co-operation means that neither country has to waste money on weapons, but each knows that if it co-operates, only to find that its neighbour has defected, it will be defenceless.

What Axelrod did was to use computing power to play long sequences of prisoners' dilemma, testing out strategies by which a player might introduce a pattern to his decisions that signalled an intention to co-operate to the second player, allowing them to optimize the joint outcome. The winning strategy turned out to be a simple one, known as tit-for-tat. The rule is to co-operate in each play or iteration of the game until and unless the other player defects. When that happens, you defect in the next round but then return immediately to co-operation. At first you lose, but the message sooner or later gets through and the long-run joint gains from co-operation wipe out the early losses. Of course, it's not a strategy to be recommended to states with weapons of mass destruction, where a single defection can call things to a halt. But it does suggest that co-operation may not be as hard to achieve as realists have claimed in more routine spheres of international relations. Political agency may not be entirely at the mercy of the anarchic structure of the state system.

This was not the view taken by neorealists, who managed at the end of the 1970s, to retain the prestige that attached to science in a world fascinated by the space race and new technology in all its forms. This was done by applying a veneer of science while dropping the essential features of positivism. There were two variants. The first, and less persuasive, was a turn to universal history. Robert Gilpin and, later, Paul Kennedy, produced grand histories of the modern states-system which claimed that some quite simple processes and cyclical patterns could be discerned beneath all the detail. The more plausibly scientific variant, explored earlier, was the theory of international politics advanced by Kenneth Waltz. Borrowing from microeconomics, Waltz proposed that all that was needed to explain the main tendencies of the states-system was to be able to ascertain the distribution of capabilities across the units in the system (that is to say the states) and to know that its anarchical structure made all states functionally identical self-help entities. But though it had much of the form of a theory, Waltz's explanation was not falsifiable. Dealing only in broad tendencies and systemic constraints, it could all too readily accommodate anomalies. Even after the dissolution of the Soviet Union, Waltz insisted for a time that the world was still bipolar, though differently so.

Since the 1990s realism has been subjected to a good deal of criticism, but it has been remarkably successful in pulling back from the extreme abstraction favoured by Waltz while retaining the systemic style of analysis on which its claim to scientific status rests. Examining historical cases and current policy has disclosed a limited palette of systemic features at work, including balancing, emulation, and bandwaggoning.

Theory, Interpretation, and Terms of Art

It has long been customary to refer to all attempts to generalize about or make sense of international relations as 'theory'. It was also customary to start any account of IR theory with the basic division between realism and liberalism (or idealism) before supplementing them with a selection, varying from one author to another, that might not include constructivism, feminism, functionalism, institutionalism, Marxism, nationalism, normative theory, positivism, post-modernism, post-structuralism, rationalism, and a bewildering profusion of sub-species of realism: classical, neo-, structural, offensive, defensive, and even neo-classical. I have deliberately restricted myself to a sub-set of -isms, briefly explaining each and avoiding the rest. Even so, newcomers may find the profusion of terms at one and the same time confusing and reassuring. It is confusing because there are so many of them, and the promise they offer of final comprehensive understanding of the ebb and flow of international affairs is illusory. And as if this were not enough, a string of sub-fields and associated disciplines awaits, the first including IPE, Security Studies, and International Organization, and the second International Law and International History at the very least, each with its own -isms. Some terms carry over from one field to another with more or less the same meaning; others change in misleading ways.

There are two good reasons, aside from sheer numbers and unfamiliarity, to be confused by this plethora, and there is sadly little prospect that the vocabulary, once acquired, will deliver on its comforting promise of comprehensive understanding. First of all, the various theories are not mutually exclusive. It is perfectly possible to be Marxist, realist, constructivist, and feminist all at once. Second, most of the -isms are not really theories at all, though some claim to be. Realism, indeed, is almost the opposite of a theory in many of its manifestations, which is what makes Kenneth Waltz's almost truly theoretical neorealism so anomalous. There is a perfectly good standard definition. A theory is a testable explanation of law-like regularities. Karl Popper insisted that a theory must yield testable hypotheses; it must be capable of falsification. Any body of thought that did not meet this criterion was mere ideology. So most of the so-called theories of IR are better classed as interpretation, conjecture, taxonomy, or universal history. Each of these methods is capable of a limited amount of work; it will not do to push any of them too hard. Each has its own corruption, which becomes apparent under stress.

Many readers forget that the sharp distinction drawn between realism and utopian liberalism or idealism in the early chapters of E.H. Carr's *Twenty Years' Crisis* was soon abandoned as Carr concluded that both were needed when analysing international affairs. The particular complementarity of realism and idealism is perhaps better conveyed through narrative than by conventional political discourse. Graham Greene's 1955 novel *The Quiet American* deals with the early stages of the war in Indo-China, when United States advisers were just starting to take over from the French. Greene (1904–91) pits his narrator, a middle-aged English journalist named Fowler, against a young American called Pyle. Fowler is contemptuous of the seeming idealism of Pyle, who arrives in Saigon claiming to have answers to all the political and economic problems of Vietnam. The young American has been reading the books of a political scientist, York Harding, of whom Fowler has heard nothing. Following Pyle's death, Fowler recalls, dismissively, that he had taken 'a good degree in – well, one of those subjects Americans can take degrees in: perhaps public relations or theatre-craft, perhaps even Far Eastern studies (he had read a lot of books).'

But neither man is quite what he seems. To hold on to his mistress, Phuong, Fowler has been willing to distort his reporting of the war and so avoid being recalled to London and his wife. Pyle's medical work is a front. As a CIA agent he encourages a local warlord, General Thé, to form a third force that may be able to restrain the Communists when the French withdraw. Pyle supplies General Thé with explosives, and a subsequent incident, witnessed by an appalled Fowler, causes many casualties to innocent civilians. But when Fowler responds by betraying Pyle to the Communists, he does not allow himself to realise consciously that this will entail the American's death and that his own motives are mixed. For Pyle's removal will prompt the return of Phuong, whom Pyle had seduced with the promise of life in the USA. Greene allows Fowler, as narrator, to undermine Pyle, but at the same time, as author, he himself reveals enough to undermine Fowler. It is a sombre little tale that led inadvertently to surveillance of its author by US intelligence services until his death nearly forty years later.

In terms of conventional international relations, Fowler is the realist who believes himself to have acquired a little practical wisdom or *nous* from experience and immersion in the local culture; Pyle, by contrast, is the idealist or liberal who 'never saw anything he hadn't heard in a lecture-hall'. (Note that Fowler is the dove, as so many realists have been, while hawkish Pyle anticipates the idealism of more recent US neo-conservatives.) In the terms set long ago by Aristotle, Fowler represents practical reason and Pyle theoretic reason, and this is why Fowler is left standing at the end to tell the story in the way he chooses, and to get the girl, while Pyle becomes, all too literally, the quiet American: 'too innocent to live'. All this time the story is being told by Greene, for whom the unnamed categories of realism and idealism are little more than a means, as they have been for many IR scholars, by which to dramatize the complexity of the world through binary oppositions.

The reason for resorting to fiction to convey a sense of the relationship between realism and liberalism is that Greene captures the essence of their relationship, which is one of mutual dependence, and does this without resort to technical language. But the student of IR will not get far by reading novels, and will sooner or later have to confront what are referred to here as 'terms of art', by which I mean words used in a technical sense within a specialized field of study.

To do this, an elementary acquaintance with some of the main divisions of philosophy is essential, because many debates in IR theory have become exercises in applied philosophy. Philosophers are often concerned with very abstract questions. Ontology asks what there is. It does not ask what is on the table or what there is in China, but what it is for anything to exist, and whether there is some hierarchy or ordering of beings in which, say, physical objects stand higher or lower than concepts or ideas. When IR scholars ask whether their ultimate object of study is the human individual, the state, or the anarchic state system, they are posing an ontological question.

Epistemology is concerned with knowledge other than our senses. It is not concerned with what the weather will be like tomorrow or whether eight plus three makes eleven. It asks whether we can rely on the knowledge we acquire through our senses, what is going on as we order that information, and whether there is any reliable source of knowledge other than the external world. Within these debates, disagreement has often been between empiricists who privilege the senses and the external world, and rationalists who point to the incoherence of raw sense data in the absence of ordering processes and categories which do not themselves derive from the external world. Methodology, for the philosopher, is more than the bundle of tools available to researchers, including statistical skills, interview technique, and familiarity with software packages. It is concerned with the more basic question of which methods are appropriate given the kind of knowledge available. When students of IR choose how to study the causes of war, they are making epistemological and methodological judgements.

So philosophy offers a scheme for thinking about what it is that is being studied, what kind of knowledge of it is possible, and how that knowledge may best be acquired. To take just one example, positivism is a methodology consistent with a rather extreme variety of empiricism.

It might seem that these issues need have no bearing on the study of international relations. The facts are out there; the problems are urgent. Sadly this is not the case. The Correlates of War project demonstrates that the facts are not simply out there. Description is not pre-theoretical. On the contrary, choices about which concepts to employ point inquiry in a certain direction from the start. Other examples of the practical importance of philosophy abound. The decision about whether to regard states as the fundamental object of study, to opt instead for the system within which states are units, or to insist on individual persons as the primary objects of study, has been identified as an ontological one. Once one level of analysis has been privileged, whether individual, state, or states-system, the range of appropriate methods narrows. There is little point collecting data about individual states if one is convinced that outcomes, such as war, are determined by the dynamics of the system as a whole. The mental condition of a statesman when resorting to force should be a matter of indifference to neorealists, but will be of the essence to a Catholic schooled in the just war tradition of practical reason. A consequentialist will think that only outcomes are morally relevant. A deontologist will hold that certain categories of action are wrong, regardless of their consequences. To hear them discuss the bombing of Hiroshima can be immensely frustrating. Until they realize the nature and profundity of their philosophical disagreement their argument will be a waste of time. To understand something of the philosophical underpinnings of debate about international relations is to start to know when an argument may be worth having and when to agree to differ, and in boardroom or bunker that may be a valuable or life-changing skill.

Take functionalism. It has never been a testable theory. Politically important for its role in legitimizing the steady intensification of economic integration in Europe since the 1950s, it is better described as a speculation about the probable effects of international organization on the power of states. Like the Latin American *dependentistas* discussed in Chapter 3, functionalists have always found some way of saving their tradition whenever it gets into trouble. Faced with repeated crises in the European project, neo-functionalists abandoned earlier expectations of automaticity and built conflict into the story. There were bound to be problems, but each successive crisis would be resolved in a way that deepened integration. Dozens of authors write of just war theory; but while there is a broad tradition riven by disagreement and a Catholic doctrine, there is, in the strict sense, no theory. Nor is globalization a theory; it is rather more an interpretation of recent tendencies, often accompanied by their extrapolation into the future and some judgement about whichever positive or negative outcomes of the process an author thinks most probable.

For anyone trying to make sense of international relations, the careful use of terms of art, an understanding of their complex origins, histories, and relationships, and a grasp of the many abstractions, assumptions, and orderings that underlie broad claims about the subject are vital. Arnold J. Toynbee (1889–1975) was director of studies at the Royal Institute of International Affairs, in London, from 1929 to 1956. There he spent half his days writing a universal history of civilizations and the other half compiling annual surveys of contemporary international affairs. He understood better than most that, without the imposition of clear concepts and structures, the present – never mind history – would appear to be 'just one damned thing after another' and that 'human affairs do not become intelligible until they are seen as a whole'. (The exact origins of these quotations, frequently attributed to Toynbee, are not clear.) A holistic vision of this kind is simply not to be had without simplification and shaping of raw experience.

To this end, I have tried in this book – while conveying essential information about contemporary international relations – to clarify key concepts and ideas, distinguishing nation, state, and territory, and considering a range of polities of which the modern state is only one. I have sought to explore liberal analyses of society and the place within them of commerce and class struggle. I have sketched the theory of comparative advantage (which really *is* a theory) and identified the conceptual pillars that support classical liberal thought. The liberal division between economics and politics and the correspondence between factors of production and social classes that provides a bridge between them are not theories, but heroic abstractions from or simplifications of reality, on the basis of which theory may be constructed. Other chapters have discussed varieties of historical writing and touched on their abuse, considered the division of history into discrete periods, paying special attention to modernity but touching also on post-modernity and dwelling on the implications of periodization for judgements about the contemporary relevance of history. I have considered a number of influential secular ideologies including nationalism, Latin American structuralism, and that peculiar fusion of nationalism and Marxism that was dependency. There have been occasional sightings of things looking very much like theory: the democratic peace, balancing under anarchy, inductivist statistical analysis of the antecedents of war, but these have mostly turned out to be chimeras.

That so many of these discussions have been more to do with abstraction, taxonomy, and analysis rather than with theory proper makes them no less important nor even less scientific, for the core of science is systematic study, with theory and prediction only one facet of this. For example, the periodic table is more a taxonomy, or ordering, of the chemical elements, than a theory proper. It was nevertheless predictive by implication; when first published in 1869 it suggested the possible existence and characteristics of elements that have since been isolated.

Aristotle drew a distinction, familiar in the early modern European world, between theoretic and practical reason. The first applied deductive reasoning to the inanimate world and has proven extraordinarily fruitful and reliable in chemistry, cosmology, and physics. The second dealt with a human world that was much less predictive because it was interactive and purposive: hence the phrase 'practical reason'. Contemporary social science, within which IR sits, is an awkward compromise between theoretic and practical reason. Sometimes, especially when dealing with large populations, social science can make good use of statistical methods. If it were not for demography, hospitals and schools would end up in the wrong place. Surveys are not always reliable, but provide some basis for planning. Yet there are many facets of society that cannot be dealt with by these methods, and they are less appropriate in the study of international relations and in foreign policy-making than in national economic management or social planning. Knowing what mix of theoretic and practical reason is appropriate in the face of political and social dilemmas is a matter of judgement. On balance IR stands more towards the practical end of the spectrum, but the high status of the hard sciences and economics has exercised a recurrent and seductive pull towards the theoretic end. In a way that both Aristotle and Thomas Aquinas would have understood, it is entirely appropriate that International Relations should be predominantly an exercise in practical reason. Lives depend on it. Yet it is equally natural that it should repeatedly aspire to theorize. International Relations has become a loose code name for studies that lean towards practice and reach out beyond states to examine economic and social relationships that cross frontiers; International Politics has consistently leaned more towards theoretic reason.

Political Science should be one contributor to a systematic study of international relations, but not its core, and both should stay in close contact with policy-making, or else face irrelevance.

Further Reading

Chapter 1 What Is International Relations?

Two books mentioned in the text have become classics, still widely read more than thirty years after their publication. Almost contemporaneous, they provide a stark contrast of method and style but, as their titles indicate, they share a preoccupation with international *politics* rather than any wider conception of international relations. These are Hedley Bull, *The Anarchical Society: A Study of Order in World Politics* (London: Palgrave Macmillan, 1977) and Kenneth Waltz, *Theory of International Politics* (Reading MA: Addison Wesley, 1979). The detail about pre-conquest trans-Andean mobility in the Southern Cone is from Kristine L. Jones 'Warfare, Reorganization and Readaptation', in *The Cambridge History of the Native Peoples of the Americas. Volume III: South America*, eds Frank Salomon and Stuart B. Schwartz (Cambridge: Cambridge University Press, 1999), pp. 138–87. The problem of the non-coincidence of state and nation is explored in Montserrat Guibernau, *Nations Without States: Political Communities in a Global Age* (Cambridge: Polity, 1999). The idea of the modern state as aspiring to, rather than ever fully achieving, sovereignty is nicely put in Richard Devetak's perceptive essay 'Incomplete States', in *Boundaries in Question: New Directions on International Relations*, eds John MacMillan and Andrew Linklater (London: Pinter, 1995), pp. 19–39. The O'Donnell quotation is from his *Dissonances: Democratic Critiques of Democracy* (Notre Dame IN: University of Notre Dame Press,

2007) p. 129. The imperfect achievement of the modern state is a frequent theme in his extensive writings. Bull's ideas are explored in Richard Little and John Williams (eds), *The Anarchical Society in a Globalized World* (Basingstoke: Palgrave Macmillan, 2006). Those of Waltz have generated many responses. Robert O. Keohane, *Neorealism and its Critics* (New York: Columbia University Press, 1986) and Barry Buzan, Charles Jones, and Richard Little, *The Logic of Anarchy* (New York: Columbia University Press, 1993) provide useful starting points. Andrew Wheatcroft, *The Habsburgs: Embodying Empire* (London: Penguin Books, 1996) provides a sense of a world in which dynasty was more important than state. For an impression of life in ethnically diverse and multi-faith Bosnia under Ottoman and subsequent Austrian rule, try the novel *Bridge on the Drinja* (London: Allen & Unwin, 1959) by Nobel prize winner Ivo Andrić, though be aware that some Bosnians complain that their Serb tormenters carried copies of it in their knapsacks during the long siege of the city (1992–96). The distinction between hard and soft power was drawn by Joseph Nye, one of the most influential writers on international relations in the USA, in *Soft Power: The Means to Success in World Politics* (New York: Public Affairs, 2004). It is to some extent a restatement of the functionalist distinction between low and high politics. The earlier book in which Nye and his co-author, Robert Keohane, laid out complementary realist and liberal views of international relations is *Power and Interdependence: World Politics in Transition* (Boston MA: Little Brown & Co, 1977). John L. Gaddis, eminent historian of the Cold War, nicely relaxed the debate about what constitutes a science in 'History, Science, and the Study of International Relations', in *Explaining International Relations Since 1945*, ed. Ngaire Woods (Oxford: Oxford University Press, 1996), pp. 32–48.

Though now dated, *Our Global Neighborhood*, the 1995 report of the UN Commission on Global Governance (Oxford: Oxford

University Press) still has useful things to say about the UN and possibilities for its reform. Michael Ignatieff, *Warrior's Honour: Ethnic War and the Modern Conscience* (London: Chatto & Windus, 1998) includes a useful and readable account of the International Red Cross, one of the oldest and most respected NGOs. The European Union has spawned an immense literature, much of it partisan. Christopher Hill and Michael Smith (eds), *International Relations and the European Union*, 2nd ed. (Oxford: Oxford University Press, 2011) place the EU in a broader context, and include a useful essay by Filippo Andreatta relating federalism and neo-functionalism to the realist and liberal traditions in IR. On TNCs, Rhys Jenkins, *Transnational Corporations and Uneven Development: The Internationalization of Capital and the Third World* (London: Methuen, 1987) is still worth reading, and provides a thorough account of the political debates surrounding TNCs from the 1960s to the 1980s. An excellent recent survey is provided by Alan Rugman (ed.), *The Oxford Handbook of International Business* (Oxford: Oxford University Press, 2009), but also consider reading one or two corporate histories to get a sense of the complex interaction of commercial, managerial, technological, and political considerations in the development of a major global corporation. James Bamberg's two volumes on BP are exemplary: *History of the British Petroleum Company. Vol. 2, The Anglo-Iranian Years, 1928–1954* (Cambridge: Cambridge University Press, 1994) and *Vol. 3, British Petroleum and Global Oil, 1950–1975* (Cambridge: Cambridge University Press, 2000). Another strong corporate history is Wayne G. Broehl, Jr, *Cargill: Trading the World's Grain* (Hanover NH and London: University Press of New England, 1992). The suggestions that the Western hemisphere international society is distinctive and that IR has lessons to learn from ethno-history derive from essays of my own: *American Civilization* (London: Institute for the Study of the Americas, 2007) and 'International Relations in the Americas in the Long Eighteenth Century, 1663–1820', in *International Orders in the Early Modern World*, eds Shogo Suzuki, Yongjin Zhang, and Joel Quirk (London: Routledge, 2013). The suggestion that attempts to modernize Egypt and the United States in response to European Great Power politics led, respectively, to the Civil War and the revolt in the Sudan is an argument advanced by Brendan Simms in several recent publications. Figures on travel and tourism are drawn from the website of the World Travel and Tourism Council at http://www.wttc.org and those for university students from the *Atlas of Student Mobility* at http://www.atlas.iienetwork.org.

Chapter 2 The Shadow of History

The first sentence of L.P. Hartley's 1953 novel *The Go-Between* (London: Hamish Hamilton) reads: 'The past is a foreign country; they do things differently there.' I make oblique reference to this at the end of the first paragraph of this chapter. The incautious comment on African history was made by Hugh Trevor-Roper, later Lord Dacre, in 1963 and then developed in an article: 'The Past and the Present: History and Sociology', *Past and Present*, 42, 1969, pp. 3–17. Of ancient historians it is the Greek Thucydides who is most often read by students of IR, and revered by some realists for his maxim: 'The strong do what they can and the weak suffer what they must.' His *Peloponnesian Wars* is available in many editions. Though its author was not the finest of Rome's historians, Ammianus Marcellinus, *The Later Roman Empire, AD 354–378* (London: Penguin, 1986) has much to offer the modern reader, chronicling the incursion into Rome's Danubian provinces of Germanic refugees fleeing Asiatic hordes, the failure of the local authorities to provide adequately for them, and the culmination of their revolt in the decisive Battle of Adrianople, in

Thrace, which marked the beginning of the end of the Western Empire. For those who prefer a condensed version, Alessandro Barbero does an excellent job in *The Day of the Barbarians* (London: Atlantic Books, 2007). Anyone disinclined to read anything about ancient history could do worse than watch Ridley Scott's *Gladiator* (2000), which conveys the scope and cultural variety of the empire and precariousness of life within it, as the action moves from German forests through North African desert to Rome itself with macabre glimpses of Spain. At the other extreme of scholarship, casting doubt on Western European and North American representations of the classical world, stands Martin Bernal's *Black Athena: The Afroasiatic Roots of Classical Civilization* (London: Free Association, 1987). The importance of the Mediterranean and the Black Sea as unifiers of the lands surrounding them is evident in John Julius Norwich's readable and comprehensive *The Middle Sea: A History of the Mediterranean* (London: Chatto & Windus, 2007) and Neal Acherson, *The Black Sea* (London: Headline, 1992). Far more profound, and with relevance beyond its chosen period, is Fernand Braudel's classic *The Mediterranean and the Mediterranean World in the Age of Philip II* (London: Harper Collins, 1992), originally published in 1949 in French, though note also David Abulafia, *The Great Sea: A Human History of the Mediterranean* (London: Allen Lane, 2011), which takes a different approach. For the medieval period, Michael Angold provides a succinct summary from the neglected heart of things in his aptly named *Byzantium: The Bridge from Antiquity to the Middle Ages* (London: Weidenfeld & Nicolson, 2001). Rosamond McKitterick's meticulous *Charlemagne: The Formation of a European Identity* (Cambridge: Cambridge University Press, 2008) is not easy reading, but demonstrates superbly the sheer foreignness of the period and the mobility and administrative grip required of a medieval emperor. Some impression of the rise of history-from-below during the second half of the twentieth century can be had from Iris Origo, *The Merchant of Prato* (London: Jonathan Cape, 1957), Emmanuel Le Roy Ladurie, *Montaillou: Cathars and Catholics in a French Village, 1294–1324* (Harmondsworth: Penguin, 1978), or – in a brief but virtuosic study summarized in the text – Rebecca J. Scott, 'Public Rights and Private Commerce: a Nineteenth-Century Atlantic Creole Itinerary', *Current Anthropology*, 48:2, April 2007, pp. 237–56. Broader in geographical scope but not dissimilar in tone and aspiration are Miles Ogborn, *Global Lives: Britain and the World, 1550–1800* (Cambridge: Cambridge University Press, 2008) and Linda Colley, *Captives: Britain, Empire, and the World, 1600–1850* (London: Jonathan Cape, 2002). The view of history as a sequence of civilizations is set out at length in Arnold Toynbee, *A Study of History* (12 vols. Oxford: Oxford University Press, 1934–61). The appeal of this weighty period piece stems mainly from its having been written alongside a series of annual reports on contemporary international relations. There is a two-volume abridgement by D.C. Somervell under the same title, which Toynbee authorized, (London: Oxford University Press, 1946–57). Should this provide too taxing, many short histories of the world are available. Depending on their political inclinations, readers may prefer J.M. Roberts, *The New Penguin History of the World*, 5th ed. (London: Penguin, 2007) or Chris Harman, *A People's History of the World: From the Stone Age to the New Millennium* (London: Verso, 1999). For an introduction to a more self-conscious school of world history that defines itself against national histories, it is hard to do better than Peter N. Stearns, *World History: The Basics* (Abingdon: Routledge, 2011). Chronological, though episodic rather than narrative, is the book based on a 2010 BBC radio series by the director of the British Museum, Neil MacGregor, *A History of the World in 100 Objects* (London: Allen Lane, 2010). Neither chronological nor narrative is the treatment of world history offered by the Uruguayan writer, Eduardo Galeano; *Mirrors*

(London: Portobello, 2009) treats world history in several hundred micro-essays. For snapshots of the Central Asian empires consult Richard C. Foltz, *Mughal India and Central Asia* (Oxford: Oxford University Press, 1998), Thomas T. Allsen, *Commodity Exchange in the Mongol Empire: A Cultural History of Islamic Textiles* (Cambridge: Cambridge University Press, 1997), which is much less narrow than its title might suggest, or Ruy Gonzalez de Clavijo, *Spanish Embassy to Samarkand, 1403–1406* (London: Variorum Reprints, 1971). Together or singly, they convey some sense of a vast and self-confident world to which Europe was peripheral. For modern Europe, Paul Kennedy's *Rise and Fall of the Great Powers* (New York: Random House, 1987) was written with an eye on the precariousness of United States power in the closing years of the Cold War. It is comprehensive and readable, providing a salutary warning against imperial overextension and the neglect of civic virtues at home. Among those who have wrestled with the exceptional resistance of Europe to political unification are Eric Jones, *The European Miracle: Environment, Economies, and Geopolitics in the History of Europe and Asia* (Cambridge: Cambridge University Press, 1981), and Jean Baechler, *The Origins of Capitalism* (Oxford: Blackwell, 1975). For a readable recent account of the British trade within the framework of the Levant Company, under charter from the English Crown, see James Mather, *Pashas: Traders and Travelers in the Islamic World* (New Haven and London: Yale University Press, 2009). The specific detail about the Eastland Company in the text is from W.K. Hinton, *Eastland Trade and the Common Weal in the Seventeenth Century* (Cambridge: Cambridge University Press, 1959), pp. 5–6. For Sidi Muhammad see Linda Colley, *Captives* (London: Cape, 2002), pp. 69, 126–32. Remarks on the poverty of Spain derive from Henry Kamen's seminal article, 'The Decline of Spain: A Historical Myth?', *Past and Present*, 81:1, November 1978, pp. 24–50. The competition between differing kinds of polity, from which the modern nation-state emerged in Europe, is the theme of Hendrik Spruyt, *The Sovereign State and Its Competitors* (Princeton: Princeton University Press, 1996). The relative importance of reduced costs of security, as against transport costs *per se*, in assuring the replacement of the old silk routes by seaborne trade is explained by Frederic C. Lane in *Venice and History* (Baltimore: Johns Hopkins University Press, 1966). A meticulous account of the triumph of inferior Manchester ponchos is to be found in Manuel Llorca-Jaña, 'To be Waterproof or to be Soaked: The Importance of Packing in British Textile Exports to Distant Markets: The Cases of Chile and the River Plate, c. 1810–1859', *Journal of Iberian and Latin American Economic History*, 29:1, March 2011, pp. 11–37, while the dismal redefinition of quality as uniformity is most poignantly chronicled, entirely without irony, in John F. Love, *Behind the Arches* (London: Bantam, 1987), a history of McDonald's. Geopolitics is nicely covered in the aptly named *Very Short Introduction to Geopolitics* by Klaus Dodds (Oxford: Oxford University Press, 2007), though it is still interesting to go back to Nicholas Spykman, *America's Strategy in World Politics, the United States and the Balance of Power* (New York: Harcourt, Brace & Co., 1942). The anglophile vindication of the efficiency of liberal states is to be found in Mancur Olson, *The Economics of Wartime Shortage: A History of British Food Supplies in the Napoleonic War and in World Wars I and II* (Durham NC: Duke University Press, 1963). It is interesting to find an echo of the old geopolitical vision in the title of Thomas W. Simmons, Jr, *Eurasia's New Frontiers: Young States, Old Societies, Open Futures* (Ithaca and London: Cornell University Press, 2008), the work of a US scholar–diplomat who commendably resists nostalgia and misuse of history in a fresh survey of the post-Soviet era. Carr drew attention to the vulnerability of small states in several of his works, but the easiest way in may be my own *E.H. Carr and International Relations: A Duty to Lie* (Cambridge: Cambridge

University Press, 1998). For Brazilian sub-imperialism see Frederick C. Turner, 'Regional Hegemony and the Case of Brazil', *International Journal*, 46:3, Summer 1991, pp. 475–509. On the universality or otherwise of balancing see Stuart J. Kaufman et al. (eds), *The Balance of Power in World History* (Basingstoke: Palgrave Macmillan, 2007). For a fuller account of the Chinese system see Victoria Tin-bor Hui, *War and State Formation in Ancient China and Early Modern Europe* (Cambridge: Cambridge University Press, 2005). For Schwarzkopf and Cannae see *The Los Angeles Times*, 27 March 1991: 'Schwarkopf Says He Hoped for a Rout of Iraqi Forces but Bush Chose to Halt War'. John Motley's *Rise of the Dutch Republic* (New York: Harper & Bros, 1855) is simply one of the best remembered and earliest of innumerable modern histories of states. The distinction between modern and contemporary history was first drawn by Geoffrey Barraclough in *Contemporary History* (London: C.A. Watts, 1964). My heart goes out to Michael Bellesiles, whose career appears to have been destroyed by a lapse of scholarship while fighting in a good cause. This is one where Google is the best starting point, but the book (still worth reading, with care) is *Arming America: The Origins of a National Gun Culture* (New York: Alfred A. Knopf, 2000). A West African cameo illustrates the ironies and frustrations on the path to authenticity. A.G. Hopkins, 'Innovation in a Colonial Context: African Origins of the Nigerian Cocoa-Farming Industry, 1880–1920', in *The Imperial Impact: Studies in the Economic History of Africa and India*, eds Clive Dewey and A.G. Hopkins (London: Athlone, 1978), pp. 83–96, is the story of West African merchants, accustomed to European dress and commercial practice, who diversified into cocoa plantations in the 1880s and felt the need to reinvent authentically African costumes for themselves. For a light-hearted fictional study of the relative importance of culture and land, it is hard to do better than Michael Chabon, *The Yiddish Policemen's Union* (New York: Harper Collins, 2007). For the keys of Palestinian refugees see Robert Fisk, *Pity the Nation: Lebanon at War* (London: Deutsch, 1990), pp.17–20. The detail on Lebanese reoccupation was in *The Times*, 10 June 2011. For a sensible account of the Yugoslav disaster that avoids primordialism see Noel Malcolm, *Bosnia: A Short History* (Basingstoke: Macmillan, 1994). Those with an interest in the region and time on their hands may still enjoy Rebecca West's *Black Lamb and Grey Falcon* (London: Macmillan, 1942), a noble attempt to elevate the travel genre into high historical art. On Spain's cautious recovery of the Civil War see Dacia Viejo *Reconstructing Spain* (Eastbourne: Sussex Academic Press, 2011) and consider the public response to Javier Cercas, *Soldiers of Salamis* (London: Bloomsbury, 2003), which rapidly became a bestseller. Ronald Maxwell's 1993 film, *Gettysburg*, is lent a poignancy that enhances Michael Shaara's 1975 novel, *The Killer Angels*, by the casting of re-enactors from the appropriate state in each regiment. The essay in which Nietzsche writes about forgetting as an aid to action is *The Use and Abuse of History for Life* ([1879] New York: Cosimo, 2005). IR scholars have been busy with 1648; start with Andreas Osiander, 'Sovereignty, International Relations and the Westphalian Myth', *International Organization*, 55, 2001, pp. 251–87.

Chapter 3 The Global Economy

For global economic history in general, Jeffry A. Frieden, *Global Capitalism: Its Rise and Fall in the Twentieth Century* (New York and London: W. W. Norton, 2006) is excellent and very readable. On the Third World challenge to the post-1945 settlement, my own short book, *The North–South Dialogue: A Brief History* (Pinter: London, 1983) is still worth reading. On the WTO and its antecedents the most succinct account is Amrita Narlikar, *The World Trade Organization* (Oxford: Oxford University Press, 2005).

For statistics, the websites of UNCTAD, the World Bank, and other international organizations are all useful. Paul Hirst and Grahame Thompson took the view that contemporary globalization was not unprecedented in *Globalization in Question* (Cambridge: Polity Press, 1996). J. Perraton, 'The Global Economy: Myths and Realities', *Cambridge Journal of Economics*, 25, 2001, pp. 669–84 provides a contrasting view. Alan Scott, *The Limits of Globalization: Cases and Arguments* (London: Routledge, 1997) offers a broad selection of essays covering cultural as well as economic aspects. Ian Clark, *Globalization and International Relations Theory* (Oxford: Oxford University Press, 1999) relates the debate to orthodox IR theory. On the origins of large international corporations see Raymond Vernon, *Sovereignty at Bay* (London: Longman, 1971). The paper in which Vernon developed the idea of the product cycle was 'International Investment and International Trade in the Product Cycle', *Quarterly Journal of Economics*, 80:2, May 1966, pp. 190–207. Rhys Jenkins, *Transnational Corporations and Uneven Development: The Internationalization of Capital and the Third World* (London: Methuen, 1987) presents one of the best summaries of the policy debate about TNCs as it stood before neo-liberalism swamped critical discussion for more than twenty years. For a more up-to-date, if less critical, view, Alan M. Rugman and Thomas L. Brewer, *The Oxford Handbook of International Business*, 2nd ed. (Oxford: Oxford University Press, 2009) is hard to beat. David Ricardo's *Principles of Political Economy and Taxation* is still widely available in cheap editions or online. Note that the three early editions vary (1817, 1819, 1821). For the history of petroleum as a key sector of the world economy, see Anthony Sampson, *The Seven Sisters: The Giant Oil Companies and the World they Made* (London: Hodder & Stoughton, 1993), or Daniel Yergin, *The Prize: The Epic Quest for Oil, Money, and Power* (New York: Simon & Schuster, 1991). Stephen Cooney, *US Automotive Industry: Policy Overview and Recent History* (New York: Nova Science Publishers, 2006) takes the story of that industry up in the mid-1970s and has the merit of extreme brevity. (After that, things get messy.) On commodity trades M. Ataman Aksoy and John C. Beghin (eds), *Global Agricultural Trade and Developing Countries* (Washington DC: World Bank, 2005) has just enough historical background to be a good introduction to the subject, in spite of its neglect of power. The chapter on coffee by John Baffes and his co-authors is cited in the text. For Immanuel Kant's view of history see his 'Idea for a Universal History from a Cosmopolitan Point of View', 1784, in *Kant: Political Writings*, ed. Hans Reiss (Cambridge: Cambridge University Press, 1991) or at (www.marxists.org/reference/subject/ethics/kant/universal-history.htm).   The quotation from Kant is in Reiss, at p. 53. Thomas Paine's *Rights of Man* (1791) is available in many editions. On Cobden, Peter Cain, 'Capitalism, War, and Internationalism in the Thought of Richard Cobden', *British Journal of International Studies*, 5, 1979, pp. 229–47, remains the clearest account. The first of the invasion-scare novels was George Chesney, *The Battle of Dorking: Reminiscences of a Volunteer* (Edinburgh & London: William Blackwood & Sons, 1871). The anti-Liberal argument is well developed in William Butler, *The Invasion of England* (1882). Both are reprinted in I.F. Clarke (ed.) *British Future Fiction* (London: Pickering & Chatto, 2001). J.A. Hobson, *Imperialism: A Study* (London: James Nisbet, 1902) was well thought of by John Maynard Keynes for its account of under-consumption and its argument for compensatory macroeconomic management by the state. Hobson's words on Jewish financial firms are from his *Imperialism*, at p. 64 in the 1902 edition. Anyone tempted to concur in Hobson's anti-Semitic view of banking should consider the role of non-Jewish finance houses in the City of London – then the world's financial capital – such as the Barings or the Morrisons. I have written about the latter family in 'Great Capitalists and the Direction of British

Overseas Investment in the Late Nineteenth Century: The Case of Argentina', *Business History*, 22:2, July 1980, pp. 152–69. Above all they should read Fritz Stern's *Gold and Iron* (London: Allen & Unwin, 1977), which shows a Rothschild connection, Gerson von Bleichröder, supporting German imperialism with reluctance, principally to retain vital domestic government accounts. 'The Imperialism of Social Classes' is the first essay in Joseph Schumpeter's *Imperialism and Social Classes* (Cleveland and New York: Meridian, 2007). It was originally published in German in 1919 as an anti-Marxist contribution to the ongoing debate about imperialism to which Rosa Luxemburg, Karl Kautsky, Nikolai Bukharin, and V.I. Lenin were all contributors. Carr first drew the analogy between the 'two scourges' in one of his *Times* editorials (5 December 1940). Many of these were later incorporated into *Conditions of Peace* (London: Macmillan, 1942). For an example of a traditional industry transformed by the Second Industrial Revolution, see Alan Dye, *Cuban Sugar in the Age of Mass Production: Technology and the Economics of the Sugar Central, 1899–1929* (Stanford: Stanford University Press, 1998). On US populism, Richard Hofstadter is still engaging; see the title essay in *The Paranoid Style in American Politics and Other Essays* (London: Cape, 1966). To understand what the farmers were up against, see Broehl's history of Cargill, cited in the further reading for Chapter 2. The easiest way into the thought of Raúl Prebisch is his *Economic Development of Latin America and its Principal Problems* (New York: United Nations, 1950). Essays by John and Richard Toye in E.J. Dosman (ed.), *Raúl Prebisch: Power, Principle and the Ethics of Development* (Washington DC and Buenos Aires: IDB-INTAL, 2006) and the journal *History of Political Economy*, 35:3, 1993, pp. 437–67 are useful. I.M.D. Little, Tibor Skitovsky, and Maurice Scott provided the most influential critique of import substituting industrialization in their 1970 book, *Industry and Trade in Some Developing Countries* (Oxford: Oxford University

Press). An impression of the style and methods of the *dependentistas* may be gleaned from early essays by Andre Gunder Frank. Try *The Development of Underdevelopment* (New York: Monthly Review Press, 1966) or *Capitalism and Underdevelopment in Latin America* (New York: Monthly Review Press, 1967). Less flamboyant is Fernando Enrique Cardoso and Enzo Faletto, *Dependency and Development in Latin America* (Berkeley and London: University of California Press, 1979). Robert A. Packenham's *The Dependency Movement* (Cambridge MA: Harvard University Press, 1992) avoids the common muddling of Latin American structuralism and the *dependentistas*, treats the emergence of dependency writing and North American reaction against it as episodes in cultural history, and is probably the most objective account of the movement. Francis Fukuyama first announced the end of history in 1989, in *The National Interest*, but then developed the argument more fully in his 1992 book, *The End of History and the Last Man* (London: Hamish Hamilton, 1992). Amy Kazmin, Patti Waldmeir, and Girija Shivakumr wrote an excellent article under the headline 'Asia: Heirs and Spares' on the *Financial Times* website, 10 July 2011, on migration, savings, and the international ramifications of Chinese and Indian bride shortages.

Chapter 4 Armed Conflict

On the Iran–Iraq war see Dilip Hiro, *The Longest War: The Iran-Iraq Conflict* (London: Routledge, 1991). On warfare in the Congo basin, see Virgil Hawkins, *Stealth Conflicts: How the World's Worst Violence is Ignored* (Aldershot: Ashgate, 2008). The Singer and Small quotation is drawn from p. 379 of a very useful book on inductivist approaches to the study of war that provided a sympathetic account of CoW techniques and achievements twenty-five years into the project. This is John A. Vasquez and

Marie T. Henehan (eds), *The Scientific Study of Peace and War: A Text Reader* (Lanham and Oxford: Lexington, 1992). Singer and Small were founders of the Correlates of War Project, and the quotation in Chapter 4 is in their book, *The Wages of War, 1816–1965: A Statistical Handbook* (New York: Praeger, 1972), p. 4. The Correlates of War project has a useful website at http://www. correlatesofwar.org. Meredith Reid Sarkees and Frank Whelan Wayman, *Resort to War, 1816–2007* (Washington: CQ Press, 2009) is a valuable addition to this literature, reflecting the recent widening of perspective. On MIDs in Latin America see David R. Mares, *Violent Peace: Militarized Interstate Bargaining in Latin America* (New York: Columbia University Press, 2001) and compare the rather different vision of Latin America that emerges, mainly from counting different things in different ways, from Arie M. Kacowicz, *Zones of Peace in the Third World: South America and West Africa in Comparative Perspective* (Notre Dame IN: University of Notre Dame Press, 1998). One of the earliest novels in English, possibly the first European war novel, came from the pen of Daniel Defoe, better known for *Robinson Crusoe*. Given the anxiety of modern social scientists about the political status of belligerents, it is interesting to find the eponymous hero of his *Memoirs of a Cavalier* ([1720] Stroud: Nonsuch, 2006) much more interested in the discipline and morale of each army than its political affiliation. On ways of war see John Grenier, *The First Way of War: American War-Making on the Frontier, 1607–1814* (Cambridge: Cambridge University Press, 2005); the My Lai quotation is on p. 224. James Fennimore Cooper nailed the issue of contrasting and conflicting ways of war long ago in *The Last of the Mohicans*. Also relevant is Max Boot, *Savage Wars of Peace: Small Wars and the Rise of American Power* (New York: Basic Books, 2002). Jean Baudrillard's infamous essays on the first Gulf War were translated into English and published as *The Gulf War Did Not Take Place* (Bloomington IN: Indiana University Press, 1995).

The video-zombies quotation is at p. 47. Those that follow immediately afterwards are from pp. 128–30 of a valuable essay called 'This is Not a War', in *Jean Baudrillard: Art and Artefact*, ed. Nicholas Zurbrugg (London: Sage 1997), pp. 121–35, written by Baudrillard's translator, Paul Patten. On the variety of kinds of warfare M. Kathryn Brown and Travis W. Stanton (eds), *Ancient American Warfare* (Walnut Creek: Rowman & Littlefield, 2003) is instructive. For the detail about Cortez and the Aztecs I have relied on Inga Clendinnen, *Aztecs: An Interpretation* (Cambridge: Cambridge University Press, 1991) and Ross Hassig, *War and Society in Ancient Mesoamerica* (Berkeley: California University Press, 1992). The literature on the democratic peace is vast. Bruce Russett has been one of the leading US inductivists, but his *Grasping the Democratic Peace: Principles for a Post-Cold War World* (Princeton: Princeton University Press, 1993) finds space for qualitative explanations as well and is therefore a good starting point. To balance it try Nicholas G. Onuf and Thomas J. Johnson, 'Peace in the Liberal World: Does Democracy Matter?', in *Controversies in International Relations Theory: Realism and the Neoliberal Challenge*, ed. Charles W. Kegley, Jr (New York: St Martin's Press, 1995), or Tarak Barkawi and Mark Laffey (eds), *Democracy, Liberalism, and War* (Boulder CO and London: Lynne Rienner, 2001). Also valuable is Michael W. Doyle, *Liberal Peace: Selected Essays* (Abingdon: Routledge, 2012). The classification of causal explanations of war by individual, polity, and system derives from Kenneth Waltz, *Man, the State and War* (New York: Columbia University Press, 1959). On the attempts of social anthropologists and sociobiologists to explain war, see the dated but useful anthology edited by Leon Bramson and George W. Goethals, *War: Studies from Psychology, Sociology, Anthropology* (New York: Basic Books, 1964), which includes William James's essay, 'The Moral Equivalent of War', pp. 21–31. Also helpful are Charles R. Beitz and Theodore Herman (eds), *Peace and War* (San Francisco:

W.H. Freeman, 1973) and Sidney W. Mintz (ed.), *History, Evolution and the Concept of Culture: Selected Papers by Alexander Lesser* (Cambridge: Cambridge University Press, 1974). The Lesser quotation is from Mintz, p. 145. My sketch of the rational choice approach to the causes of war is heavily indebted to James D. Fearon, 'Rationalist Explanations for War', *International Organization*, 49:3, Summer 1995, pp. 379–414. The classic neorealist account is Kenneth Waltz, *Theory of International Politics* (Reading MA: Addison Wesley, 1979), but there is also a short and more precisely focused essay by Waltz on 'The Origins of War in Neorealist Theory', in *The Origin and Prevention of Major Wars*, eds Robert I. Rotberg and Theodore K. Rabb (Cambridge: Cambridge University Press, 1989). On the law of war see L.C. Green, *The Contemporary Law of Armed Conflict*, 3rd ed. (Manchester and New York: Manchester University Press, 2008); on its evolution, Stephen C. Neff, *War and the Law of Nations: A General History* (Cambridge: Cambridge University Press, 2005). Thomas E. Ricks paints a glowing but plausible picture of the US Marines in *Making the Corps* (New York: Simon & Schuster, 1997). For the detail about US lawyers and the revival of the just war tradition see Christopher R. Rossi, *Broken Chain of Being: James Brown Scott and the Origins of Modern International Law* (The Hague and London: Kluwer Law, 1998). The standard modern work on the ethics of war is Michael Walzer, *Just and Unjust Wars: A Moral Argument with Historical Illustrations*, 4th ed. (New York: Basic Books, 2006). For more orthodox Christian treatments see James Turner Johnson, *Can Modern War Be Just?* (New Haven and London: Yale University Press, 1984) or Oliver O'Donovan, *The Just War Revisited* (Cambridge: Cambridge University Press, 2003). Phillip W. Gray, *Being in the Just War* (Saarbrücken: Verlag Dr. Müller, 2007) is a remarkable book deserving wider distribution than it has received. The work of Carl Schmitt has been popular recently with the European Left in spite of his commitment to the Nazi regime. Schmitt's *The Nomos of the Earth in International Law*, trans. G.L. Ulman ([1950] New York: Telos Press, 2006) is probably the most important twentieth-century German work on international relations. A good sense of the scope and concerns of military ethics, as distinct from state-centric treatment of the ethics of war, can be had from textbooks designed for the staff colleges and military academies and monographs by some of those who have worked there. In an anthology on *Ethics for Military Leaders* (Needham Heights MA: Simon & Schuster, 1998), Aine Donovan and his co-editors cover the entire range of approaches to ethics, with excerpts from classical and modern authors – including practitioners, novelists, and academics – organized into fourteen sections. The just war is only one of these fourteen. In their *Military Ethics: Guidelines for Peace and War* (Boston MA and London: Routledge & Kegan Paul, 1986), Nicholas Fotion and G. Elfstrom took a similarly comprehensive view. By contrast, C.A.J. Coady and Igor Primoratz organized a collection of reprints, *Military Ethics* (Farnham: Ashgate, 2008) more timidly into three sections, of which the first two corresponded to *jus ad bellum* and *jus in bello*; but the third, under the title 'The Soldier's Ethics', raised questions of military virtue, honour, and the like. James H. Toner, who served in the US army between 1968 and 1974 and saw action, has taken a virtue ethics approach at the US Air War College in Alabama, and this is clear from his *Morals under the Gun: The Cardinal Virtues, Military Ethics, and American Society* (Lexington KY: University Press of Kentucky, 2000). Timothy L. Challans, in *Awakening Warrior: Revolution in the Ethics of Warfare* (Albany: State of New York University Press, 2007), fears that 'the ghost in the military machine is asleep at the wheel'. Finally Nancy Sherman, a philosopher who has spent time at the US Naval Academy, examines the points of contact between contemporary United States military ethics and classical Stoicism in *Stoic Warriors*

(Oxford: Oxford University Press, 2007) while Elizabeth D. Samet has written perceptively about the encounters of her West Point cadets with imaginative literature in *Soldier's Heart: Reading Literature through Peace and War at West Point* (New York: Farrar, Straus and Giroux, 2007).

Chapter 5 Making Sense of International Relations

Davies laid out his plan for a multinational force in considerable detail in *The Problem of the Twentieth Century: A Study of International Relationships* (London: E. Benn, 1930). With matchless grasp of national stereotypes he allocated the navy to Britain, artillery to the Germans (so good at technology and science), and the air force to the Italians who, after all, could claim in Leonardo da Vinci the designer of both monoplane and helicopter. But Davies' master stroke was to place the headquarters of his force – a new District of Columbia – in Palestine. Who could object? One long-serving member of the Aberystwyth department put it nicely. Reading Davies, he mused, one began to see 'the squire of Llandinam and Master of Foxhounds in a novel yet curiously familiar role: allotting tasks, sizing up the country, planning new and exciting types of hunt to extirpate the vermin and predators of the world'. The quotation is on pp. 61–2 of an essay by Brian Porter in David Long and Peter Wilson (eds), *Thinkers of the Twenty Years' Crisis: Inter-War Idealism Reassessed* (Oxford: Clarendon, 1995), a useful collection that subverts the stereotypical version of the period peddled by E.H. Carr. Of Mitrany's many works see *A Working Peace System: an argument for the functional development of international organization* (London: RIIA, 1943). Leonard Woolf, husband of the novelist Virginia Woolf, is best remembered within IR for *International Government* (London:

Fabian Society, 1916), a 'project … for a supranational authority that will prevent war'. Pre-1914 intimations of IR have been reported in numerous publications by Duncan Bell and Casper Sylvest, notably Bell's *Idea of Greater Britain: Empire and the Future of World Order, 1880–1900* (Princeton: Princeton University Press, 2007) and Sylvest's *British Liberal Internationalism, 1880–1930: Making Progress?* (Manchester: Manchester University Press, 2009). E.H. Carr's *Twenty Years' Crisis: An Introduction to the Study of International Relations* (London: Macmillan 1939, 1945, 2001) had some of its less palatable phrases cut from the postwar edition. It is interesting to compare the two, as Michael Cox does in the 2001 third edition. Often classed as a realist, Carr nicely illustrates the difficulty of such classifications, being sensitive to the inseparability of economic and political affairs, a firm believer in the possibility of progress, and author, in Chapter 6 of *The Twenty Years' Crisis*, of what remains one of the most devastating critiques of political realism available. These contradictions are explored in my 1998 book on Carr, listed in the further reading for Chapter 2. The surprising realism of the British Labour Party's Foreign Policy Advisory Committee is explored in Casper Sylvest, 'Interwar Internationalism, the British Labour Party and the Historiography of International Relations', *International Studies Quarterly*, 48:2, June 2004, pp. 409–32. Francis Boyle puts the argument about international law as a soft power resource for the USA before 1914 in *Foundations of World Order: The Legalist Approach to International Relations, 1898–1922* (Durham NC: Duke University Press, 1999). Other useful modifications of the standard narrative of IR and its reliance on past thinkers include Brian C. Schmidt, 'On the History and Historiography of International Relations', in *Handbook of International Relations*, eds Walter Carlsnaes et al. (London: Sage, 2002), pp. 4–22, David Long and Peter Wilson (eds), *Thinkers of the Twenty Years' Crisis: Inter-War Idealism Reassessed* (Oxford: Clarendon, 1995),

Miles Kahler 'Inventing International Relations: International Relations Theory after 1945', in *New Thinking in International Relations Theory*, eds Michael Doyle and G. John Ikenberry (Boulder CO: Westview, 1997), pp. 20–53, and Charles A. Jones, 'Christian Realism and the Foundations of the English School', *International Relations*, 17:3, 2003, pp. 371–87. For a standard account of the two intellectual traditions, realist and liberal, see Chapter 2 of Charles W. Kegley, Jr and Shannon L. Blanton, *World Politics: Trend and Transformations* (Boston MA: Wadsworth, 2010–11). Martin Wight's trio are set out in his *International Theory: The Three Traditions* (Leicester: Leicester University Press for the RIIA, 1991). Wight uses the term 'rationalism' eccentrically; for its standard philosophical sense see John Cottingham, *Rationalism* (London: Paladin, 1984). Chris Brown et al. (eds), *International Relations in Political Thought: Texts from the Ancient Greeks to the First World War* (Cambridge: Cambridge University Press, 2002) is an anthology providing sufficiently extensive excerpts to enable the student to begin to question the neat allocation of European thinkers to schools or traditions. Among the heralds of IPE were Charles Kindleberger, *Power and Money: The Economics of International Politics and the Politics of International Economics* (London: Macmillan, 1970) and Klaus Knorr, *Power and Wealth: The Political Economy of International Power* (London: Macmillan, 1973). Textbooks followed, notably Joan Edelman Spero, *The Politics of International Economic Relations*, 7th ed. (Boston MA: Wadsworth Cengage Learning, 2010), first published in 1978, and Robert Gilpin, *The Political Economy of International Relations* (Princeton: Princeton University Press, 1987). The contributions of Hirsch and Strange were rather more oblique. Fred Hirsch, *The Social Limits to Growth* (Cambridge MA: Harvard University Press, 1976) is essentially a work of economic sociology. Susan Strange's *States and Markets* (London: Pinter, 1998) nicely and deliberately eschews abstraction (economy, polity) in favour of institutions, leaving open the possibility of a material–base/ institutional–superstructure analysis. Benjamin J. Cohen has provided a useful history of IPE: *International Political Economy: An Intellectual History* (Princeton: Princeton University Press, 2008). Among the grander sort of sociologist to have acquired an IR following, Immanuel Wallerstein and Manuel Castells stand out, the first for *The Modern World System* (New York: Academic Press, 1974), his account of multiple world-systems based on exchange finally coalescing into a global system, and the second for *Information Age: Economy, Society and Culture* (Oxford: Blackwell, 1996–8), his novel and monumental analysis of globalization. Herbert Butterfield deals with deterrence in 'The Tragic Element in Modern Conflict', one of the essays in his *History and Human Relations* (London: Collins, 1951). Neorealist works of a historical nature (though the second is not explicitly realist) include Robert Gilpin, *War and Change in International Politics* (Cambridge: Cambridge University Press, 1981) and Paul Kennedy, *The Rise and Fall of the Great Powers* (New York: Random House, 1987). The most entertaining edition of Graham Greene's *The Quiet American* is surely the one in the Viking Critical Library (New York: Penguin, 1996). In a volume that seems to have been edited by Pyle himself (under the pseudonym of John Clark Pratt), Greene's text is dwarfed by critical apparatus. On Greene's politics see Anthony Burgess, 'Politics in the Novels of Graham Greene', *Journal of Contemporary History*, 2:2, 1967, pp. 93–9. For the encounter between inductivists and *dependentistas* see Steven Jackson et al., 'An Assessment of Empirical Research on *Dependencia*', *Latin American Research Review*, 14:3, 1979, pp. 7–28. For one of the best essays on the distinction between theoretic and practical reason, see Lord Rochester's 'Satyr on Mankind'. There are many editions, but Penguin's *John Wilmot, Earl of Rochester: The Complete Works* (1994) is useful, as it includes some of the lewdest verse of the notoriously lewd Restoration era, a kind of party bag for the reader who has made it right to the end.

Acknowledgements

More than any other book I have written, this one reflects the experience of teaching. It is through preparing and delivering a great variety of courses on North–South Relations, International Political Economy, the European Union, Comparative Regional Integration, Business History, Transnational Corporations, International Relations Theory, World Politics, the History of International Society, and the Ethics of War, by examining in departments of History, International Relations, Latin American Studies, and Development Studies, and by attending seminars and conferences to hear about the research of students and colleagues that I have received a general education in International Relations over the years. Like many IR scholars of my generation I never studied the subject formally, and I was not at all sure what it was when first appointed as a lecturer at the University of Warwick. The absurdly small size of that department and the freedom and stimulus with which Barry Buzan and I, as junior scholars, were allowed to graze by an indulgent Robert Skidelsky, brought rewards that would have been much harder to come by in a larger and more disciplined outfit. We formed a kind of academic commando, operating behind disciplinary lines without clear guidance, causing sporadic damage, though nothing too serious.

While writing this book I have frequently found myself thinking of the work of postgraduate students I have taught, advised, or examined. Some are mentioned in the section on further reading; others will recognize fleeting references to their unpublished work; still others have had a more subtle influence, through conversation. My particular thanks go to

Tanya Kamchomnong, Alex Anievis, Ricardo Soares de Oliveira, Duncan Bell, Casper Sylvest, Benjamin de Carvalho, Juan Pablo Scarfi, Andrew Tillman, Paul Seccaspina, Eddy Fang, and Lisa Smirl, but this list could easily be extended. Ed Rushton read the whole of an early draft and made valuable suggestions. I also wish to thank Steve Bloomfield, Helen Skaer, and Margaret Caistor. Study leave from the University of Cambridge provided the opportunity for me to draft the book, but that absence placed additional burdens on colleagues, especially Duncan Bell, Brendan Simms, and Geoffrey Edwards.

The book would not have been completed to schedule without a period of concentrated work in total isolation during the summer of 2011 in which I neglected Linda, Kate, and Alex. They have at all times been a great source of support and encouragement.

Cambridge, July 2013

Index

Note: *f* following a page number indicates a figure